EXPLORING WOODS

Also available
in this series:

PONIES AND YOU
Sue Turner

THE WILD WEST
Robin May

Have fun with
ORIGAMI
Robert Harbin

S.O.S. WILDLIFE
true Survival stories
Victor Edwards

IS THERE LIFE IN OUTER SPACE?
Peter Fairley

EXPLORING WOODS

PETER SCHOFIELD

Independent Television Books Ltd, London

INDEPENDENT TELEVISION BOOKS LTD.
247 Tottenham Court Road
London W1P 0AU

© Peter Schofield 1975

ISBN 0 900 72735 7

Printed in Great Britain by
Tinling (1973) Ltd, Prescot, Merseyside
(a member of the Oxley Printing Group)

CONTENTS

Foreword
by Elizabeth and Anthony Bomford

We have always lived in the country, and until we came to make a programme about British woodlands for Anglia TV's Survival series I suppose we thought we knew quite a bit about the woods round our home. But as we got further into the film we realized how much we didn't know about the fascinating mosaic of life that goes to make up the wood. We would never have guessed the vast number of small mammals there. The voles among the ivy, the shrews at home in the nettles, and the woodmice scuttling at darkest night across the bare leaf mould in the very heart of the wood. In order to film anything we had to develop rather nocturnal habits ourselves. We stalked nightingales, and tracked down tawny owls. On warm spring mornings we just sat still, very still, and waited. The wood takes a long time to settle down after someone has walked through it — perhaps an hour or more. Gradually things return to normal. Just as you are about to either give in and go home, or grow roots, things begin to happen. A deer wanders across the glade in front of you, a bank vole investigates your wellington boot.

Most of us in Britain have access to woods of one sort or another. They may be well-trodden places of public recreation, or perhaps off the beaten track, remote and overgrown. In this book Peter Schofield leads us enthusiastically and lucidly into the complex natural history of woodland habitats, and yet his treatment of the subject is so thorough that although the book is broadly based to encompass all types of wooded country it is detailed enough to answer the mass of questions that inevitably arises if you 'take another look'. Of course, that's just what Peter wants us to do, because to care for and preserve our wild places we must know them very well indeed. There is no doubt that in the next few years what little woodland we have will be under great pressure from a public seeking recreation, from property developers and from farmers wishing to claim land for agriculture. Certainly our wild areas will not resist this tide unless there is a hard core of people who care, prepared to defend wooded areas that are strategically important in wildlife's struggle for survival.

There's a great dearth of knowledge about many important woodlands. You certainly don't need to be a scientist to make a substantial contribution – simply keep your eyes open and systematically take notes along the lines explained in this book. One of our local nature reserves, for example, has been painstakingly documented from the botanical point of view, but virtually nothing is known about the small mammals. We once asked what sort of bats were to be found in the wood and were told 'none'. Of course, this is highly unlikely, and so even this wood, close to Cambridge University and well trodden by eminent naturalists, offers scope to the young enthusiast looking for a project. County Naturalist Trusts, the Royal Society for the Protection of Birds, and your local Bird

Club will all help (See page 123 for addresses) and will give school parties access to their reserves where possible. If you are going it alone, there are frequently reduced membership fees for students.

A Birch wood

INTRODUCTION

On a clear sunny morning in April many sounds come from the wood. A wren is singing; another sings not far away — are these two male birds defending their territories? A great tit calls. A wood pigeon 'claps' its wings as it takes off from the upper branches of a tree and this sound echoes through the still morning air.

The leaves on some trees are opening before others. The horse chestnut is coming into leaf; so are the elder and birch. The oak is not yet in leaf. At the top of one tree is a large collection of sticks — is this the nest of a magpie or a carrion crow? Somewhere in the wood a green woodpecker calls with his distinctive 'laughing' notes. The shrill, high-pitched 'zee-zee-zee' of the goldcrest pierces the morning air. The wood is long and narrow and as the leaves are not fully out you can see through to the far end. In the top layers of the trees the twigs form a dense crown. Under them are crowns of smaller trees. Below the smaller trees are shrubs. The trees are of many ages: young saplings, middle-aged trees and old trees with many dead branches and with a number of holes in the trunk where old branches have fallen off.

A sycamore at the edge of the wood has not opened out its leaves; another, deeper in the wood, has buds at the top of the tree but nearer the bottom the leaves are partly opened. Why should this be? Ivy is climbing up some trees but not up others. The elm is just bursting into leaf. Some trees have a green growth of algae on only one side of the trunk — why? There are lichens on some trees but not on others — why?

Walk slowly towards the wood so that animals or birds that may be feeding in the field alongside the wood or just inside the boundary hedge are not disturbed.

Through the gate at the edge of the wood there are patches of bare soil among the dead leaves. Could this be where pheasants have been scratching for food? Are there any signs of footprints? Overhead the alarm call of the blue tit can be heard, 'chur-r-r, chur-r-r'. Perhaps it has a nest nearby. Sit down for a few minutes and look, listen and smell the air. The bluebells are just coming into flower. The sun throws patches of light between the shade cast by the tree trunks. How important is sunlight to woodland plants and animals? A path or track winds through the ground vegetation. Has this path been made by animals or by man? That should be easy to discover as there are probably some footprints along the track.

There are groups of ferns in the wood; a patchy carpet of ivy; plenty of dead sticks, useful for nest-building; on some of the sticks mosses are growing; and foxglove plants, not yet in flower.

The barks of trees have many different textures. That of the birch is different from that of the elm, which in turn is different from the sycamore and from the oak. Some of the bluebell leaves have been nibbled — what creature has done this? The wood is full of living things:

earthworms, flies and other insects, spiders, woodlice, chaffinches, coal tits, treecreepers, mistle thrushes, willow warblers and a sparrowhawk.

In less than an hour forty-eight different observations have been made. all within the first 10 metres of the wood. There is too much information to handle, and more questions are being asked than answered. Observations are being made in a random fashion and very little appears to relate the first observation to the second.

But occasionally two or three things in succession are clearly related to each other. For example the alarm call of a wren is followed by the alarm call of a chaffinch, then a sparrowhawk skims through the wood. As the sparrowhawk feeds on small birds, it is hardly surprising that you heard the small birds warning one another.

In some ways understanding a woodland is like doing a jig-saw puzzle. At first you have nothing but a box full of pieces. In order to discover what the picture is like you have to look at the pieces, sort them out and arrange them in order. The more pieces you can fit together the clearer the picture becomes. Now there are many different ways in which you can start to look at a woodland. It does not matter too much where you start, providing you remember that you are trying to join together the various bits of information you collect.

As there is so much of interest you should define your objective quite clearly. You may wish to spend two or three days in a wood before you finally decide which aspects you would like to study first. For instance you may want to look at birds, or you may prefer plants. Perhaps you will choose to look at trees, their distribution in the wood and the order in which they come into leaf.

Sparrowhawk — a woodland predator

9

1
THE WORLD OF THE WOOD

Many woods contain a wide variety of plant and animal life. Monks Wood, a nature reserve near Huntingdon, gives some indication of this variety.

The wood is thought to be the remains of an ancient ash and oak woodland typical of many that used to grow on clay lowlands in England. Over 370 different kinds of flowering plants and ferns have been recorded there. There are nearly 100 different liverworts and mosses, 34 lichens and about 350 fungi. The wood contains a vast array of insects, with over 120 kinds of plant bugs, 85 species of frog and leaf hoppers, 18 lacewings, at least 44 butterflies and over 400 moths, about 300 different kinds of flies, 17 species of flea, over 170 sawflies, ants, bees and wasps, and over 1,000 different species of beetle! So far only 122 different kinds of spiders have been recorded here but there are probably many more. Here, too, 16 of the 21 British harvestmen, or porters which are relatives of the spiders, have been found. Mites and ticks add another 140 species to the list. Also found here are 13 of the 44 British millipedes and 9 of the 44 centipedes. Over 40 different types of snails and 12 different earthworms make the tremendous total of over 2,500 different kinds of invertebrate animals. There are 12 kinds of reptiles and amphibians in the British Isles and 10 of these have been seen in Monks Wood. It is known that 57 different kinds of birds have bred in the wood, and a further 58 species have been seen. Completing the list are 25 different kinds of mammals.

Monks Wood, however, is a little different from most woodlands in that it is a National Nature Reserve, which has been selected as a reserve because of its wildlife. It also has the benefit of a near-by research station, so that scientific experts are able to work in the wood. But the number of plant and animal species gives some indication of the richness of British woodlands and this should encourage you to seek out a woodland's secrets for yourself. Of course not all woodlands will be as exciting as Monks Wood. You need an army of experts and considerable time to identify this number of plants and animals — people have been collecting and recording plants and animals in Monks Wood for over 150 years.

You need not identify all the plants and animals in a wood; but you must learn about the major groups of plants and animals and the various parts and layers of the wood. With this knowledge, you can see how each plant or animal helps to build up the woodland picture.

PLANT SUCCESSION

Why do some areas grow into woodland while others do not? Bare ground never stays bare for long. Weeds grow and are followed by other kinds of plants. Find some newly dug ground and notice what happens. Note the plants that appear first and then observe how long they survive before other plants take over. Often the first plants to grow have a delicate structure, and are frequently swamped by later arrivals that are more robust. This process, by which one hardier type of plant takes over from a weaker one, is known as plant succession. Grasses often take over from the first weed colonizers. When there are sheep, cattle or rabbits about, the vegetation usually remains as grassland, which often contains a selection of creeping herbs that grow close to the soil and can survive the nibbling.

In the 1960s the rabbit disease, myxomatosis, brought about changes to the vegetation in many parts of the country. For example Newborough Warren in Gwynedd was an area of sand dunes and coastal grasslands on which thousands of rabbits lived. The disease killed most of the rabbits so there were only a few grazing animals to check the growth of grass or to eat off the tops of seedlings. The grasses therefore grew unchecked and eliminated some of the more delicate flowering plants. Some hawthorn seeds, probably dropped by birds, fell into the grasses and began to grow. As there were no rabbits to nibble the young hawthorn seedlings, they continued to grow into bushes.

On an area of mountain grassland in Wales, and on some chalk grasslands on the Chilterns, fences were erected to keep out sheep. After a few years the vegetation within the fenced area had changed completely — shrubs and small trees had appeared in the grasses. Woodland is often the vegetation that comes at the end of a plant succession, and is called climax vegetation.

CLIMAX VEGETATION

The climax vegetation over much of Britain would be woodland if there were no grazing animals and no people. Once the climax vegetation has been reached it tends to stay for a long time. In prehistoric times the climax vegetation usually changed because of a major change in climate, whereas nowadays man frequently brings about the changes.

ECOSYSTEMS

How do woods differ from other types of vegetation that cover the earth? Think of some large expanses of apparently uniform vegetation and describe them. Some of the most obvious will be farmland and parkland. Apart from these you might describe mountain grassland, heather moor, heath, marsh, chalk-hill grassland, sand-dune vegetation, salt marsh or woodland. Each of these major types of vegetation, together with the soils on which they grow and the animals they contain, is called an ecosystem.

How would you describe the most obvious feature of the woodland ecosystem? You would probably say that it contains larger plants (trees) than other ecosystems. It is sometimes difficult to see where some of the other ecosystems begin and end, but it is easy in the case of the woodland ecosystem, as woodlands in Britain tend to have definite boundaries. Even so, occasionally woodland grades into scrubland, which in turn grades into heath and finally grassland.

What is special about the woodland ecosystem? The most noticeable feature is the large number of plants and animals that depend upon the shelter and security of woodland for many of their daily needs. Never think of trees as just trees (or wood), but as part of a biological system in which trees, other plants, and animals live together and affect one another. Think of each wood in terms of a home for various plants and animals. Every plant or animal prefers a special type of wood in which to live, or a particular part of the wood (its habitat). By knowing more about woodland structure you will be able to find out something about plant and animal habitats.

FOOD CHAINS

All animals and plants need food in order to live. Many animals, known as herbivores, rely on plants for food. Others, known as carnivores, feed on the flesh of other animals. When one animal feeds on another the killer is called a predator and the killed is called the prey. A blue tit could feed on a greenfly, which in turn would feed on the sap of a plant. We might write it like this: plant — greenfly — blue tit.

This process is known as a food chain. A simple food chain of this type can be extended: soil minerals — plant — greenfly — blue tit — sparrowhawk.

If we work out several food chains, it will become obvious that all animals find their food directly or indirectly from plants, and that most plants, especially grasses and leaves of herbs, shrubs and trees, provide food for some animal or other.

Charles Darwin, in a fascinating book called *Vegetable Mould and Earthworms*, described how worms pull dead leaves into the soil by their stalks. The rotting leaves later provide food for the worms.

Each layer of woodland vegetation provides food for a wide variety of butterflies. The dog violet, which is common in many woodlands, is the food plant for the caterpillar of several species of fritillary butterfly. Bramble provides food for caterpillars of the holly blue, green hairstreak, and grizzled skipper butterflies; blackthorn for the brown hairstreak and the rare, black hairstreak butterflies; the elm for caterpillars of the large tortoiseshell, camberwell beauty, white-letter hairstreak and comma butterflies.

FOOD WEB

But life is not quite so simple as the food chains just described. Food chains represent only a small part of the very complex relationships between plants and animals. Think about an animal at the end of a food chain: the sparrowhawk in the second example feeds not only on blue tits but on house sparrows, chaffinches, greenfinches, redwings, song thrushes and many other species of bird. Similarly the blue tit will feed not only on greenflies but also on the caterpillars of many insects. And then again it is not the only predator on the greenfly: ladybirds, for instance, eat vast numbers of them.

If you make careful notes of your observations you can begin to draw up a food web. Start by connecting the various food items by means of lines showing the links between predator and prey. Then trace the links back to plants. The food web is called a food cycle or food network by biologists.

FOOD PYRAMID

It is no good being a predator like a fox, sparrowhawk or buzzard if there is not enough prey (food) to see you and your offspring through the year. In order for the species to survive, the size of the population of small birds preyed upon by a sparrowhawk will have to be large enough to provide food for the predator and leave enough birds over to maintain its own species. If a sparrowhawk were to feed on one small bird a day, there would have to be 365 birds available just to keep one sparrowhawk alive for a year. But that is still not enough. Enough small birds must be left over at the end of the year to lay eggs to carry on their own species and to continue to provide another 365 birds as food for the sparrowhawk during the next year. But then of course the sparrowhawk will itself produce young, so the total number of small birds required each year will be enormous.

Now think of the vast quantity of insects that would be required to feed all these small birds. It has been estimated that one pair of great tits, for example, will eat 7,000 to 8,000 insects, chiefly caterpillars, in about 3 weeks! Similarly if the insects are to survive, they must have enough food in the form of plant leaves. On average it takes about 7 kilograms of food in the form of vegetation to produce 1 kilogram of animal. Or for 1 kilogram of sparrowhawk there will be about 7 kilograms of small birds, 49 kilograms of caterpillars and 343 kilograms of vegetation.

LIMITS TO GROWTH

Many factors can limit plant or animal growth or the number of animals in a woodland. One overriding factor is climate. For example consider the effects of a severe winter on birds. As the ground becomes frozen, worms, spiders and insects become more difficult to find. Seeds become frozen in the ground and are difficult to dig out. If there is a covering of snow much of the available food will be hidden. Ponds become frozen and fish-eating birds like the heron will not be able to reach food. If hard weather continues for any length of time a large number of birds die. This is illustrated by the effect of a severe winter on the herons in Tabley Wood in Cheshire.

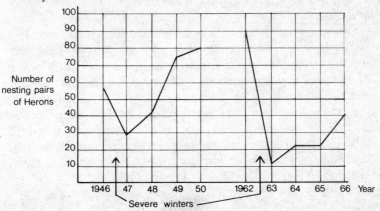

STIMULUS TO GROWTH

Favourable weather can help to increase animal populations. After a number of years with no serious summer drought and mild winters, all kinds of animals will increase in numbers and their predators will also be able to survive in larger numbers throughout the winter. By 1974, after a number of mild winters, the numbers of many birds, particularly the smaller ones such as long-tailed tits, goldcrests and blue tits, increased considerably.

Besides climate and food, four of the most important factors affecting animal populations are: shelter or cover — to give protection from predators and from the wind and the cold; suitable places for breeding; disease; and pollution.

OTHER WOODLAND RELATIONSHIPS

We should always be looking for patterns in nature, and for relationships between animals and plants. A food is not the only network that we can piece together. For example, mistletoe is dependent upon finding branches of trees on which to grow and upon having birds to carry its seeds to a new position.

Many lichens are so small and delicate that to survive they have to grow on tree trunks and obtain food from rainwater trickling down the trunk. In this way they overcome the problem of surviving in competition with the more rapidly growing grasses and flowering plants of the woodland floor.

Fungi, such as bracket fungi, and wood-boring insects like the caterpillar of the goat moth can kill a tree. This new situation provides an interesting range of possibilities for other fungi and for animals such as woodlice. In the early stages of decomposition bark may become loosened and the tree creeper will nest behind the dead bark. When the tree has fallen woodlice and centipedes will live under the dead bark and several species of fungi will begin to grow on the dead timber. Holes in tree trunks provide nest sites for many birds ranging from the blue tit to the tawny owl.

2
THE WOODLAND YEAR

The pattern of life in a woodland changes from month to month. In the winter most things are fairly quiet. Many animals hibernate through the cold winter months. As the days begin to get warmer and longer, the first flowering plants begin to appear. Most of us look for the first snowdrops in spring. Herons and rooks — both birds that nest in colonies — start to build their nests in the tops of trees early in the year. As the year progresses and the buds begin to unfold, insects, which have largely been dormant thoughout the winter, begin to become active. Young caterpillars and many insects will feed on the new leaves. As caterpillars begin to grow, the eggs in many bird nests begin to hatch. There is now a plentiful supply of caterpillars and newly hatched insects for the adult birds to feed to their young.

As the size of caterpillars and the numbers of insects reach their height so the birds that have been spending the winter in warmer climates around the Mediterranean and in Africa arrive to build their nests. Their young hatch out at a later date than those birds that have spent the winter in Britain so they are not in competition for the same caterpillars.

As autumn approaches all the larger woodland animals begin building up stores of food for the winter. Squirrels and wood mice stockpile nuts, while migratory birds eat large quantities of food to build up body fats that they will use as fuel on their long migration back to the warm sun. Several animal species also build up supplies of body fat so that they can use it as food and insulation against the cold during their long winter hibernation.

As the leaves begin to fall off the trees the first winter migratory birds, the redwings and fieldfares, arrive from the far north. By October layers of fallen leaves cover the ground and start decaying and the many types of woodland fungi begin to appear. The year ends much as it began with most things quiet in the wood.

JANUARY

Days are at their shortest in January and so day-time feeders, particularly birds, seek food from dawn to dusk. Birds tend to hunt in flocks and so are not as evenly distributed throughout the wood as they are in the breeding season. The easiest way to locate them is to stand still and listen for their continuous calling and twittering. Soon you will locate a party of birds. Sometimes, you will find, they are all of one species or even of one sex. Separate flocks of hen and cock chaffinches, for example, are quite usual. Other flocks may be mixed and you frequently find groups of blue tits, coal tits and great tits feeding together.

The time of day also influences bird behaviour. If you visit a wood towards evening you may find flocks of birds coming into the wood to roost. The most likely examples are jackdaws, rooks, fieldfares, redwings and song thrushes. Starlings frequently roost in vast numbers. By watching the flight patterns of jackdaws and starlings in the late afternoon you can locate their roosting areas. You may have many surprises in winter woodland expeditions. Mistle thrushes are usually seen in pairs, or perhaps in a family party. But in the winter, like many other thrushes, they will often gather together and forty or fifty of them may be seen flying into a wood at dusk. Sometimes the blackbird — another bird that you usually find in small numbers — can be seen feeding in quite large parties at the edges of woodlands during the winter months.

Perhaps the best place to look for predatory birds is in or near a wood used by smaller birds as a roosting area. Sparrow hawks frequently hunt starlings, redwings or song thrushes. I have several times seen kestrels trying to surprise finches and sparrows looking for warm roosts in ivy-covered trees. As the light begins to fail tawny owls and, if you are lucky, long-eared owls can be seen hunting for food. Near woodland edges barn owls and little owls may be seen.

Wherever there are large flocks of roosting birds you are likely to see tracks of a fox. An early-morning visit may reward you with the sight of the dog fox or vixen returning from a night's hunting. This is also the time of year to listen for the scream of the vixen. January is a good time to look

18

for animal tracks as the ground remains soft for several days following rain. If there is snow on the ground this will also help you to track animals and birds.

Woodland plants are not much in evidence, although you may see tips of snowdrop shoots or the first shoots of dog's mercury appearing through the bare soil.

FEBRUARY

February can be a month of varying weather conditions. Warm, mild spring-like days can be preceded or followed by heavy falls of snow. It is interesting, therefore, to try to compare the activity in the wood throughout the month and relate this to the weather.

Use a pathway or some other easily distinguishable route through a wood and try to cover this on several occasions during the month. Note down the species of birds you see and the numbers of each. You can also record any other animals or evidence of animals that you see or any plants that are flowering.

Some of your woodland birds may leave if there is severe frost or snow. They will try to find alternative food supplies in areas that are generally milder than the wood in which they usually live. But don't forget that for a short period of time the picture may be complicated by similar movements of birds flying in from the Continent.

The Rook begins to repair old nests in February

Some species of birds begin their courtship and nesting activities as early as February. Some woodland birds that nest in colonies, particularly the heron and rook, are already beginning to repair old nests and begin the process of laying eggs and rearing young.

Are any birds still using the woodlands near your home for roosting during February? If so, which species and roughly how many of each kind? Do the birds come to the same roost night after night or do they seem to use different woods on different occasions?

Is there any evidence of woodland animals? Look for tracks in the soft ground. Other signs may be the remains of eaten cones and nuts or, in heavy snows, grazing animals will turn to eating tree bark instead of ground vegetation. Can you find any evidence of this?

Plants such as the bluebell, dandelion and cuckoo-pint are beginning to open their leaves.

If the weather is particularly hard you may find barn owls hunting during the day on the edges of a wood or even a tawny owl hunting through the wood before dusk.

MARCH

Now you should start to look for the first spring flowers. Towards the end of the month look particularly for dog's mercury, primrose, violet, anemone and celandine. Which of the shrubs or under-storey trees are in flower in March? Many woodland birds will start singing on the milder days of the month. Try to detect the song of the robin, mistle thrush, blackbird and song thrush.

At the end of the month you may hear the first chiff-chaff. It has a song that sounds like its name, chiff-chaff, chiff-chaff, chiff-chaff.

APRIL

The warmer sun, longer hours of daylight and April showers will bring about major changes in most woods. In woods where the wild strawberry grows you will be able to find it in flower, along with the tiny moschatel, carpets of bluebells and wood sorrel. Buds on the trees will be opening out (check the order in which they appear), and the greys and browns of the winter woodland will erupt into a sea of greens.

Some of Britain's resident birds, like the mallard or wild duck, blackbird, robin, thrushes and wren, will be making their nests now. In the tree tops the magpie and carrion crow will be sitting on their eggs. In April the chiffchaff will be singing more often and you will frequently hear two or three singing at the same time.

In April there will be a rush of other summer-visitor birds: willow warbler, blackcap, whitethroat (at present quite scarce) and redstart.

By the end of April one of the most welcome calls of all can be heard — that of the cuckoo. The cuckoo is not a woodland bird but it can often be heard in forests with scattered trees or in heathy or scrubby areas.

Butterflies have not really started to appear but four brightly coloured species that may be seen on warm days are the brimstone, orange tip, peacock and small tortoiseshell.

MAY
May is the month for insects. The small heath, pearl-bordered fritillary, marsh fritillary, red admiral, small tortoiseshell, peacock, comma, holly blue and wood white are some butterflies on the wing in May. In addition to but-

The Green-veined White — on the wing in May

terflies there are numerous woodland moths, hatching from their pupae. There is not much point in many of these insects hatching earlier because there would be few leaves on the trees on which to lay their eggs, and for their young caterpillars to feed on.

Now that butterflies and many other insects are on the wing it is the turn of the insect-pollinated flowers to bloom. The crab-apple, broom, common maple, hawthorn, rowan, spindle, holly and bramble are some of the plants that flower in May.

The hedgehog has now built up his strength after his winter sleep and times his breeding season to coincide with the rapid growth of many invertebrates on which he feeds. The main breeding season of the deer family is also in May and June, while in the pine forests of Scotland the first young of the wild cat will be born.

April and May are the months when one of the sounds most associated with woodlands can be heard. Drumming, the loud vibrating sound made by both male and female great spotted woodpeckers, echoes through the wood. The sound is made by a rapid rain of blows with the bill on a dead trunk or branch, which acts as a sounding board.

One interesting sight in May is the 'roding' of woodcock. The woodcock is a bird with a long bill, something like a snipe, that lives in woods with damp soils. On May evenings just before dusk the woodcock will fly round and round his wood, calling as he goes. Sometimes two or even three woodcocks will perform this special breeding-season flight.

Late spring bird visitors such as the pied flycatcher, wood warbler, garden warbler and the nightingale will have arrived from Africa, where they spend our winter. Now is the time to learn their song. These species, with the exception of the garden warbler, have a restricted distribution, so find out from a bird atlas, book, or ornithologist whether they occur in your district before you go looking for them.

The first few hours of daylight spent in a deciduous wood on a warm sunny May morning are one of the most pleasurable experiences you can have. The experience can be even more memorable if you get up an hour before dawn and arrive in the wood before the dawn chorus. The dawn chorus is difficult to describe; it has to be heard. All the birds of the wood begin to sing their territorial songs. First the robin may start, followed by the cuckoo, the mistle thrush and a host of others.

JUNE

The summer sun is now here and many woodland animals are at the height of their activities. Caterpillars of butterflies and moths and the larval stages of many beetles and other insects spend all day, or in some cases all night, eating their way through tons of leaves. Greenflies suck sap from the leaves and stems of plants. Ants hurry back and forth collecting food for their colony, and bees and wasps are enlarging their nests.

Meadow brown and ringlet butterflies are hatching from their pupae and many species of moth are on the wing as the warm evenings turn to dusk. The large reddish-brown cockchafer beetle, which feeds on the leaves of trees and shrubs, is a common evening flyer.

Nightingales, blackcaps and garden warblers are singing from the thickets. In more open woodlands, particularly in southern England, the turtle-dove purrs away.

Hedgehog

Just as the leaves of the trees cut out much of the sunlight from the lower layers of the wood so the same leaves often make it difficult for us to see what is going on in the canopy. Many insect-eating woodland birds will be up there finding food for their nestlings. Many more young birds will have recently left the nest and will themselves be looking for insects.

Some of the later flowering shrubs will be coming into flower. Dogwood, wild rose, honeysuckle, privet and elder are some mid-summer flowers that are insect pollinated.

One of the most unusual sounds to listen for in June is the churring call of the nightjar. This bird of the pine woods and heaths is more common in the south than the north. Visit a heath or hillside with groups of pines on a warm evening early in the month. Keep quiet and, if you are lucky, just before dusk the nightjar may start his call.

JULY

Although summer holidays are beginning, the year is now halfway through and days are already becoming shorter. The ground is warm and grass snakes slide through the ground vegetation, while lizards may be seen basking on sun-warmed rocks.

There are still many species of butterfly on the wing and you may perhaps see the first purple and white-letter hair-streaks.

Many woodland mammals are introducing their young to the wider world by July. Badgers, foxes and polecats will be searching for food with their young. The deer will have finished their breeding season, though many other mammals will still be breeding. If you are going on summer holidays to North Wales or Scotland, look for these animals. Often stoats, weasels, foxes and some of the other nocturnal animals will search for food in the daytime, as their rapidly growing young will often need more food than can be gathered during a night's hunting. There is plenty of food about, for plants have grown the maximum amount of foliage and there are many young birds and animals for predators to feed on.

Fruits are beginning to ripen on several tree and shrub

24

species, although the main bulk of seeds and fruits will not be ripe for about another two months.

AUGUST

Many plants both in the shrub layer and the under-storey' are producing fruits; this is especially true of the 'soft' fruits, such as bramble, elder, honeysuckle and yew.

The red admiral butterfly attempts to hibernate through the British winter, but very few survive our frosts. But each spring many red admirals that have spent the winter in France migrate to our shores. They lay their eggs on stinging nettles and by August we see the adult insects. It is perhaps even more surprising that this butterfly reaches the Faeroes, a small group of islands between Shetland and Iceland in the North Atlantic. The small tortoiseshell and the peacock are two butterflies that hibernate throughout the winter in the adult stage. Both lay their eggs on stinging nettles at the edge of the wood or in a woodland glade. In August they will be seen on marsh thistles or on the fruits of blackberry or elderberry.

Most birds will have finished nesting but some will still have their young in the nest. Birds that have two, three or sometimes four broods in a year, such as the song thrush and blackbird, will be rearing their last ones. Several birds of the finch family will also be bringing up their young.

Of the later flowering plants, foxgloves and white campion can still be found.

Before the widespread use of agricultural pesticides (insecticides) on arable crops, grasshoppers and crickets could be heard over most of Britain on a hot August day. Nowadays you may have to go to those parts of Britain where sheep and cattle are the main types of farming to hear grasshoppers. Woodland edges, away from areas of arable farming, are also good spots to hear the grasshopper's 'song'.

SEPTEMBER

September is the month for berries, fruits and seeds. Hawthorn, rose hip and holly berries add a touch of brightness to the fading greens of the leaves. Alder seeds, hazel nuts and

Moss capsules

juniper berries all ripen now. Winged fruits of the sycamore, beech 'mast' and many cones of spruce, larch and pine produce ripe seed. The beautiful wayfaring tree's red berries turn to a deep purple as they ripen and the feathered seeds of traveller's joy begin to decorate many woodland edges. Both these plants can be seen along many miles of our country roads.

With the abundance of food, most birds and animals will be eating or storing as much as they can. Many birds are preparing for the long migrations to warmer lands. They must build up large reserves of fat as the flight may be 5,000 – 6,000 kilometres long. Many migratory birds, such as flycatchers and warblers, that leave our woods at the end of summer are insect eaters and will be tucking away as many of the larger caterpillars or insects as they can find.

The woods begin to lose their wood warblers, blackcaps, willow warblers, garden warblers and redstarts, while the villages lose their swallows and house martins.

The mistle thrush will be having a feast of the hedgerow and under-storey berries. The red squirrel will be eating and storing nuts before winter sets in.

The first winter visitors. which are avoiding the snows and

ice of Scandinavia, northern Europe or Iceland, are beginning to arrive — redwings come with fieldfares, and in some years vast eruptions of waxwings arrive in our woods. Sometimes more sparrowhawks will appear from Scandinavia.

In many cases the jig-saw puzzle is difficult to solve. For example, in September large numbers of woodcock arrive from western Russia, the Baltic States, northern Germany and Scandinavia. These birds will add to the numbers of our own woodcock that have built their nests and brought up their young in Britain. But some British nesting woodcock will migrate to Ireland, while others go to France, Spain and Portugal.

When most birds have stopped singing the robin begins his autumn song, which now rings through the woods without competition from many other species.

OCTOBER

Winter bird visitors continue to arrive. Many chaffinches arrive from the continent of Europe and with them there will often be some bramblings. The brambling is particularly fond of beech mast. The nuthatch, a colourful woodland bird, will feed on many seeds at this time of year, although it is an insect eater in the spring and summer. You may be lucky enough to see the nuthatch taking hazel nuts, beech mast or acorns. Many other woodland birds that eat insects in spring and summer will turn to eating seeds in autumn. The great spotted woodpecker for example will eat similar seeds, plus those from coniferous trees.

We have nearly all seen great tits and blue tits coming to garden bird tables and eating seeds in winter. In the wild these birds will eat many different seeds once the young have left the nest. Blue tits have been seen eating birch and Scots-pine seeds as well as pecking at beech mast. The marsh thistle and several kinds of small seeds are eaten by the coal tit.

October is the best month to start looking for fungi. The bright colours and interesting shapes of this group of plants give added interest to a woodland visit. You can search for fungi anywhere, on fallen leaves, grassy patches, soil, dead branches and tree trunks. You will find them in all kinds of

Fungi on decaying Birch log and on leaf litter

woods in all parts of the country.

If you search the leaves of the sycamore tree you will probably find many black spots and blotches. These spots are also a kind of fungus that attacks sycamore leaves.

The landowners of many woods will 'tidy up' the wood in October. Hedges surrounding the wood will be trimmed and 'laid', a process by which the main hedgerow stems are partly cut and bent over to form a more solid barrier. Ditches will be cleared out so that the winter rains will drain away.

NOVEMBER

Another good month for fungi. Now that most of the leaves are off the trees, the winds, especially those from the north and east, leave you in no doubt that winter is here. Few flowers bloom and you may find a few seed heads still holding their seeds. Many birds, particularly goldfinches, greenfinches and chaffinches, will eat these. And many species collect in flocks in winter to search for food or to roost.

Flocks of blue, great and coal tits will search the wood. Long-tailed tits usually remain in parties of their own species, although sometimes they join forces with other tits.

Many birds roost in the wood but hunt in the fields away from the wood. Towards dusk these birds will return. Fieldfares and mistle thrushes will make their way into a thicket. Wood pigeons gather in flocks and roost in thick woodland. Large numbers of crows, jackdaws and rooks noisily settle in some woods. You may be able to plot the flight path of these birds as they make for their roost against a clear November sunset. Magpies, another member of the crow family, also gather together to roost in the winter months, although their flocks are never as large as those of the rooks and jackdaws. The jay, which is the most faithful to woods of all the crow family, may also be seen in small groups of up to seven or eight birds. But the most spectacular sight of all is a big starling roost. An hour or more before sunset excited flocks of these birds will gather in the fields near to their roost, before finally flying to their nightly home.

Food is often scarce so in the hour or more before dark you may see the white barn owl hunting along the woodland margins or through woodland rides. The little owl, no bigger than a blackbird, also hunts before dark or may continue to look for food after dawn has broken. The little owl prefers the smaller wood, particularly one that has many rabbit burrows, which it uses for roosting and nesting in.

One of the rarest British owls is the long-eared owl. Of all our owls, this species is perhaps the most closely associated with woodlands. It is particularly attracted to conifer woods. If you should come across one, having recognized the prominent ear-tufts on top of the head, tell your local natural history society because they will probably be very interested.

On a still November evening, an hour or two after dark, listen for the call of the tawny owl, a 'hoo-hoo' or 'hoo, hoo-hoo'. This call can be heard from October until late spring in many town parks as well as in wooded countryside.

The tree creeper, a tiny brown and white bird, can often be seen most easily at this time as he searches for insects and spiders in crevices in tree bark.

By now many woodland animals are hibernating: bats in holes in trees; hedgehogs rolled tightly in a ball in a collection of dry leaves under a fallen tree; snails often together under a stone, in the soil or in rotting timber. Several butterflies — the small tortoiseshell, peacock, comma and brimstone — hibernate in a hole in a tree, in some old building or in the gaps of a dry-stone wall.

The only woodland plant in flower in November is the ivy. Look closely at the flowers and the developing fruits.

DECEMBER

Woodland in December is much the same as in November. If there has been a fall of snow, then tracking woodland animals will teach you some additional facts about life in the wood in winter. Hares may take shelter in the wood and, if the snow remains for several days, grazing animals will often be forced to eat the bark of young trees. Can you find any signs of this?

The winter moth appears during the period November to January, sometimes earlier or later depending upon the climate. This unusual moth is generally found throughout

Hoar frost

the British Isles. It is unusual because the female is almost wingless and can't fly. She crawls up the tree after she has hatched from her pupa. The male is not a very spectacular moth, with his greyish-brown forewings, which have darker lines crossing them and a distinct central band.

It seems strange that several insect-eating mammals do not hibernate when their food is probably at its lowest availability. Shrews, for instance, keep searching for food throughout the winter and moles also continue their hunt for worms and insects. In snow you can often see fresh brown mole hills above the snow or long humps of snow where the mole has 'burrowed' in the snow or under the surface of the ground. Look at mole hills carefully: often you will see footprints of blackbirds and robins in the snow around them. The mole has done them a good turn by turning up some fresh soil that may contain food.

Although we have gone the full cycle of twelve months and looked at each month separately we should remember that in the woods December will slip into January with no sudden change. It is not of course 31 December that is the important changing-point, but the length of day, the temperature of the soil and the air, the strength and direction of the wind and the amount of rainfall.

3
HOW TO BEGIN TO STUDY A WOODLAND

First select a suitable wood that is not too large, say, between 1 and 5 hectares. If possible the wood should have several areas dominated by different tree species. It is important to choose a woodland near to your home or within easy reach of public transport. The more you find out about your wood the more interesting it will become and the more you will wish to go there. Next it is essential to ask the owner's permission before you start to explore his wood. Tell him what you wish to do and show him the plans you have made. He may say no for a number of reasons — he may be using the wood for game rearing or have just planted out a large number of seedlings. He may say the wood is being used as a nature reserve and he wants to keep disturbance to a minimum. Don't be upset if the first wood that you have selected is not available for study. If the

A woodland scene. Note the dense ground vegetation

owner is a large landowner he may be able to suggest another woodland in which you will be able to work.

Next study the Country Code and make sure you know it thoroughly and the reasoning behind it. Also remember the Outdoor Studies Code whose main points are:

> **plan and lead excursions well**
> **take safety seriously**
> **choose and use your area carefully**
> **respect ownership**
> **think of other users of the countryside**
> **leave the area as you found it**
> **avoid disturbing plants and animals**
> **do not collect unnecessarily**
> **safeguard rare species**
> **give no one, man or animal, cause to regret your visit**

If you do not make good relationships with those who use the land for farming, forestry or other purposes you will jeopardize your future visits and those of others who may wish to study later.

Always think about the safety aspects before you start. Let people know where you are going and when you expect to be back home. Look out for hazards such as steep, slippery banks, rocks, dead or decaying trees, soft ground, and such things as old mine shafts or wells. If you have an accident anywhere it is bad enough, but if you are in the middle of a wood it may be some time before anybody is aware that you are in trouble. Always carry additional clothing for warmth and protection against rain. It is always advisable to carry a whistle, particularly if you are working alone.

Before making any expedition, whether it be up the Amazon, to the South Pole or to your own woodland, you should plan it properly. First decide what your objectives are. Your first objective will probably be quite simple, such as to find out more about the plants or the animals that live in your chosen woodland.

You may find you like to explore your woodland with two or three friends. If so you may decide that each of you will look at a different aspect of the woodland and then together build up a picture of the wood. Whichever way you start it is very important to take great care over your observations and the making of field notes. Make observations by listening, looking, smelling, touching and occasionally tasting. Note down your observations, ask questions about the facts you record. Why has something happened? What is the relationship with the surrounding features of the wood? Have you made similar observations before, or is this a new observation? What part does the observed activity play in the life of the woodland? When you have thought out some of the answers and indeed some new questions you can look for other situations in which you might expect to make similar observations and then check to see if this is the case.

When you start your study don't rush into it but spend the first two or three visits simply walking about the wood making observations and noting down interesting features. At the same time get a rough idea of the geography of the wood. Try to obtain a 6 or 25 inch to the mile Ordnance Survey map of the area. These are expensive so you may have to borrow one from a friend or the library before you can make a rough sketch map of the outline of your wood and of any features in the wood that are marked on the map.

If you have been to the wood before you may already have some questions in mind. If you have not been to the wood before, make your first visit an exploratory one.

Once you have selected your problem — for example, how many different tree species grow in the wood? — you can then ask yourself some additional questions. Are the trees evenly distributed or are there clumps of different kinds in different parts of the wood? Is there any pattern of tree distribution? Do certain species grow near special features such as streams or steep slopes?

You must now decide how you are going to study your problem. You may decide to describe different parts of the woodland, or you may wish to map the distribution of trees or to make a transect (see page 66).

MAKING A MAP OF YOUR WOOD

For any study, making a reasonable map of your wood is very important and it is well worthwhile taking some care over it. Some simple maps can be made using protractors if you have an understanding of map-making. But this is more difficult in woodland because it is not easy to get the long views that you have in open country.

The first thing to do is to make a basic description of the wood. You can start by describing the location of the wood, its shape and size. The size can be gauged approximately from a 1 : 50,000 or a 1 inch to the mile Ordnance Survey map (1 km. sq. on the map is equal to about 100 hectares or 250 acres) or from the 25 inch Ordnance Survey map on which acreages are shown (some sheets are now produced on the 1 : 2,500 scale and have areas of land shown in hectares and acres). You should now describe the physical features of the woodland.

Once you have collected these details they will be valid for the rest of the survey, unless some major disaster, such as severe flooding, alters some of the features. The main physical features you can record are the height above sea level (taken from a 1 inch Ordnance Survey map), the slope of the ground, the aspect of the wood (direction the slope faces) or various parts of the wood (does it face south or east? etc.), and the general nature of the area (flat, hilly, a steep-sided hill, low-lying swampy or marshy ground). You can also map and describe the type of land that surrounds the wood.

Before you go too far with your study it is a good idea to check how other people have done similar studies. You won't want to do exactly the same study in the same wood as somebody else — that would probably be a waste of time. But you may want to do a similar study in your wood and compare your results with those of some other researcher in a different wood. If you decide to do a comparative study of this sort it is very important that you use exactly similar methods. So study their methods carefully and follow them.

When you are reading make a list of references, as these will be useful both throughout the study and for years to come. Your list of references could be like those in the book-list at the end of this book.

It is a good idea to buy some index cards and keep one card for each reference. These can be stored by authors' surnames in alphabetical order. As your list of references expands you can store them in sections by subject — for example you may want to keep all the plant, animal, bird and general woodland references separate.

In addition you could check with your biology master, the local museum, a local university or technical college department, a field centre or a natural history society to see whether they have any information about the wood you have chosen or about the particular aspects of your project.

It is always a good idea to work out a method before you start your study. Have a list of the items you will need on each visit. Develop your own system for making field notes.

The next stage will be to write down your selected method and then have a trial run to see whether you have been able to collect the information that you hoped.

Give some thought to how you are going to present your investigation. Are you going to use maps, tables, graphs, drawings, photographs or just written material? A rough idea of how you may finally present your information can make the collection of field data more efficient and meaningful. It is always infuriating to find that you have one vital bit of information missing when you come to write up an experiment or piece of research.

You are now ready to start the expedition. Let's hope the weather is sunny for the first trip. As you approach the wood, long before you enter it, stop, look and listen. A hen pheasant may run from the field back into the wood. Is it nesting? There is an important point to be made here. Although you would naturally like to find out more about the pheasant, remember that it is a game bird that could easily be disturbed and prevented from rearing its young. As pheasants are a source of income to some landowners, you will have to leave this bird in peace.

A DESCRIPTION OF A SELECTED WOODLAND

If you want to describe the main areas of woodland by their dominant trees, make a tracing of your woodland map. Then visit the wood and, using the symbols on page 38, mark the tree species on the map. Obviously you cannot mark every tree so you have to simplify the task by marking the boundaries of areas of similar trees.

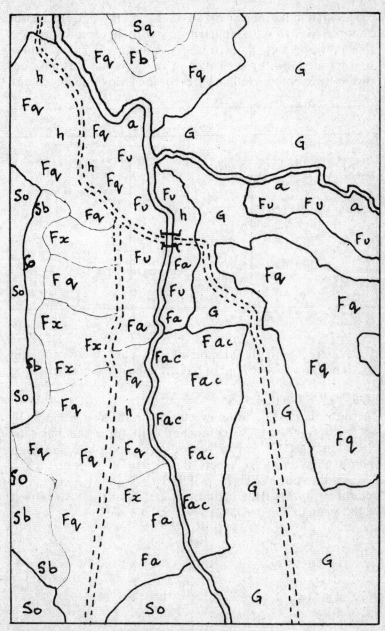

SKETCH MAP SHOWING GROUPING OF TREES IN A WOOD
For key to letters see table on page 38

This system has been worked out by the Biological Records Centre at Monks Wood that will give you a letter code for each area of woodland. Select one letter from each box, where appropriate, and for each part of the woodland. It may not always be easy to include a letter for the type of management.

Major Habitat Type	Type of Wood	Type of Management or Man Made Features
F Forest — woodland S Scrub. D Dwarf shrub T Tall herb (>2ft) G Grassland and short herb (<2ft) B Moss dominated E Marginal habitats (edge) O Open habitats (vegetation cover less than 25%)	a Alder k Sweet chestnut x Ash f Beech b Birch u Elm h Hazel z Sycamore r Hornbeam l Larch q Oak p Pine w Willow y Yew t Poplar & aspen o Other	y high forest c coppice n coppice with standards p plantation h hedgerow v roadside verge b embankments or cuttings u. walls
	d deciduous* c coniferous* m mixed*	

* These symbols can be used with the species and the code letter should always come before the species code letter.

An example of a description of one part of a woodland might be F q n (woodland of oak coppice with standards).

FOR PLANT STUDIES
The information you are now putting on the sketch map will be useful for years to come and will form the basis of several studies. On copies of your base map you can map certain plants and see where they occur in relation to the features on your sketch map. This exercise may help you to determine some of the conditions that limit the distribution of the plants.

4
CLOTHING AND EQUIPMENT

The only equipment you have used so far has been a notebook and pencil. Wide-awake senses and notebook are in fact by far the most valuable equipment you need. Once you can rely on making good observations and logical deductions, you can then consider using a wide range of aids to assist you in your woodland studies. Some of this extra equipment is fairly inexpensive, but some of it can cost quite a lot of money. The type of equipment you buy will depend upon what you particularly want to study.

WHAT KIND OF CLOTHING?
It is important to make sure you have the right kind of clothes. A strong pair of shoes or boots is essential if you are to remain comfortable throughout a visit that may last several hours. In many woods, particularly alder and willow woods, which grow only in damp conditions, a pair of wellington boots is useful. But even with wellington boots you should be particularly careful where there is a lot of alder or willow about. On many occasions water has gone over the top of my wellingtons in the wetter patches of such woodlands!

In winter plenty of warm clothing is required, as you may be standing about in a cold wind for a considerable time. You will need a pair of gloves, a woollen hat and a waterproof anorak, preferably with a hood. There is nothing more frustrating than to find you are frozen or soaking wet just as your observations start to become exciting.

If you are buying new clothing for your outdoor activities make sure the colours are similar to those of your surroundings as this will help you avoid being seen by animals. Greens, browns, greys and blacks are best. Additional pockets are useful; these can be sewn on to the inside of an old jacket or on to the front of the thigh in an old pair of trousers. The pockets can be made to take a standard-size field notebook or pens and pencils and a pocket ruler. A poacher's pocket on the inside of the lower part of an anorak or jacket can be useful for carrying certain specimens or types of equipment.

A small rucksack is a useful item, especially if the weather is changeable and you don't want to wear your waterproofs and extra warm clothes straightaway. But do beware of carrying too much equipment for comfort.

NOTEBOOKS

You can buy notebooks with waterproof covers but these tend to be expensive. Notebooks with squared paper are useful if you regularly count up large numbers of birds or animals or if you want to make sketch maps. Never use a fountain pen for your field observations because you will find that drips of rain make your writing or figures illegible. Ball-point pens are generally much better, although in very cold weather they have a horrible habit of seizing up just when you want them most! Pencils on the other hand are much more reliable — as long as you don't break the point! Make sure your pencil is not too hard or it will not show up well in field notebooks. An *HB* or *B* is about right.

CHECK-LISTS

A number of organizations produce field check-lists of plants, animals and birds. For example the Biological Society of the British Isles (BSBI) produces a plant check-list. The British Trust for Ornithology (BTO) and the Royal Society for the Protection of Birds (RSPB) produce similar lists for bird species. You can now buy printed lists for almost any group of animals or plants. If you want to study a particular group, and you think printed lists would help, ask your science teacher or the secretary of a local natural history society for details. Check-lists do have their uses, but you will find that if you just tick off the plants or birds as you see them you will never have any practice in making good field notes.

Most check-lists have room for several visits and they are also useful for comparing one site with another. But even if you do use check-lists you will still have to make notes for a general description of the site and write down the date, the weather and possibly the time of the visit, plus any other unusual observations. Don't forget that if you use the check-lists together with your notebook you will have to be very careful that you can cross-refer from one to the other.

One last point on check-lists and field notebooks. They will contain all your information built up over many field visits so don't lose them. It is wise to leave completed cards at home or to copy your field notes out before your next visit. In this way, if you should lose your notes, at least you have got most of the information safely duplicated at home.

TAKING FIELD NOTES

Get into the habit of making field notes. You will be surprised how many details escape your memory once you get home. If you don't make notes you will find you will be unable to remember whether that moth had five red spots or six red spots on the forewing and this will be just the characteristic you need to identify it. There is nothing more annoying than to be asked what colour rump a small bird had and not to be able to remember. It is surprising how often a small detail will be the key to making a positive identification of an insect, bird or flower.

WOODLAND DIARY

It is a good idea to keep a woodland diary. You can have great fun collecting and making illustrations for it and it has the added advantage that you will always be able to add something to your notes even after a short visit to a woodland. But do plan one or two projects that you can undertake at the same time as keeping up your diary.

MAPS

The 1 : 50,000 or the one inch to the mile Ordnance Survey maps are very useful for finding your way about and locating the position of woodlands. A 1 : 25,000 (2½ inches to mile) map of your particular district or the area in which you work is also useful. The larger-scale maps are really useful only if you wish to do more detailed work on the distribution of plants or birds within your study area.

FIELD GUIDES

There are now field guides or inexpensive books on almost every branch of British natural history (pages 120-3).

RECORDING BOARD

If you want to make some drawings or to do some simple map or survey work a recording board is very useful. Recording boards can be bought but it is much more fun to make your own. The size of the board should be a little larger than a standard A4 size (25 cm x 35 cm), so that there is a margin round your paper.

You can add many refinements to your recording board. For instance a transparent plastic envelope attached to the back is useful for keeping spare papers or a map. You can also buy clips for your board so that spare pencils can be attached.

HAND LENS AND FIELD-GLASSES

A hand lens for use in the field is a good investment as it enables you to obtain as much detailed information as possible for your field note-taking. If you want to watch birds, field-glasses are essential. Before buying a new pair consult an expert bird-watcher or read one of the guides about buying them. They are an expensive piece of equipment so it is important that you get the right glasses for your own requirements. For instance field-glasses for use in woodlands need to be very different from those that you would use for watching birds on estuaries; if you are going to use glasses regularly in open country as well as in woodland then a pair midway between the two is probably the best buy.

SPECIMEN CARRIERS

A selection of waterproof polythene bags will help to keep your field notebook or pocket guide dry. Polythene bags are also useful for carrying certain types of specimens.

A variety of containers can also be improvised: plastic bags for mosses; tubes, tins, matchboxes or small jars for beetles and insects; a large tin with blotting paper, newspaper or plastic bag for plants; jars or tins with good lids for soil, and plastic yoghurt, cream or honey cartons for fungi. All kinds of specialist equipment can be bought from one of several dealers — for example, you can get boxes with glass tops for insects, or tins with perforated tops and a special opening in the side for caterpillars.

Labels are essential. With their help you can number any specimen you find and jot down the number in your notebook so that full details of your observations can be related to the specimen once you get home.

So much collecting of specimens has been carried out in the past that some species of British plant or animal life are becoming difficult to find. You should check the legal position as a number of Acts of Parliament forbid the collection of such things as birds' eggs. Instead of making your own collection visit museums, which often have extensive collections. Only a minimum number of specimens should be taken for identification or research.

Other useful items of equipment are a trowel, a pocket knife, a tape measure and nets for catching insects. Portable tape recorders or a camera can provide interesting additional records in some instances but it isn't easy to take good photographs in many woodland situations.

For some activities a hide will be a valuable piece of equipment. You can make a portable hide or buy one from a supplier. In some cases you can build a semi-permanent hide near to a regular bird or animal drinking place or close to the nest or den of a bird or animal. Always take great care not to disturb the animals or birds and seek advice before you start. You must also of course get permission from the landowner.

The rest of your equipment will depend upon what type of fieldwork you want to do. It is unwise to buy a lot of equipment straightaway, so aim to collect items over the years.

5
WHAT IS A TREE?

You may think this is an easy question to answer, and in many ways it is. Trees are plants — but so are seaweed and snowdrops! What is different about trees? They are the largest plants growing on earth and they have woody stems or trunks, most of which grow to at least 5 or 6 metres in length. In fact the main difference between a tree and other plants is that trees have the ability to grow trunks and branches of woody material that increase in width year after year.

If we think about the plant kingdom in a little more detail, we discover that there are two main kinds of plants: those that have flowers (flowering plants) and those that don't (non-flowering plants).

The non-flowering plants contain such groups as ferns, mosses, liverworts, fungi (including moulds, mushrooms and toadstools) and algae (including the seaweeds, many of the

Trees grow woody trunks and branches

44

green growths found on tree trunks and the green slimy filaments in ponds). Although they reproduce themselves in a great many ways, non-flowering plants do not produce seeds from which new plants can grow. There are usually a number of non-flowering plants like ferns and mosses in most woodlands

Flowering plants are equally varied and include grasses, rushes, herbaceous plants like buttercups and daisies, shrubs such as privet, and trees. The flowering plants are further divided into two main classes: the gymnosperms, which embrace all the main cone-bearing or conifer trees, such as pines, firs, spruces and larches; and all the rest — the angiosperms — which include grasses, herbs, shrubs and trees such as the oak, elm, ash, beech and birch. The flowers of many tree species are not very colourful; they do not all have bright petals like bluebells and roses and often they are greenish in colour (like hazel catkins).

The leaves of trees in the two main classes are different too. Most conifers have needle-like leaves, whereas the angiosperm trees have broad, flat leaves.

The conifers are known as softwoods, whereas broad-leaved trees are known as hardwoods. Flowering plants, including trees, are made up of millions of tiny parts called cells. The wood of hardwoods contains long cells called vessels, which carry water and other substances from the roots through the trunk, branches and twigs to the leaves. In older trees only the newest part of the wood (the outer part) is really active and transports sap up the trunks. That is why the outer part is often called the sap wood. The inner part of the tree consists largely of vessels or cells that have filled up with a hard substance called lignin. These non-living cells make up the heart wood. In some hardwoods such as the oak and ash, vessels are formed at different rates. When growth is slow in autumn and winter small vessels are formed, in spring and summer much larger vessels are produced. In each year, therefore, there will be a double ring of growth within the tree. By counting the rings on a tree trunk that has just been cut down, you will be able to tell how old the tree was.

A hardwood tree also has fibres, from which the tree gets its strength, and radiating medullary rays, which store the nutrients that it will need for new growth in spring before the leaves are fully opened. The medullary rays give the wood of trees like the ash and oak their characteristic grain.

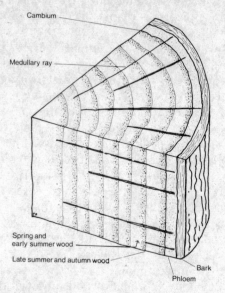

DIAGRAMATIC SECTION THROUGH PART OF A LOG FROM A HARDWOOD TREE

Cambium

Medullary ray

Spring and early summer wood

Late summer and autumn wood

Bark

Phloem

Towards the outside of the tree is a thin layer of cells called the cambium. Every year the cambium makes new vessels from its inner surface and produces phloem cells or bast from its outer surface. The thin layer of phloem or bast carries materials that have been made in the leaves back to the trunk and roots. Round the outside of the tree is a protective layer of bark.

In softwoods cells called tracheids conduct water and nutrients up the trunk as well as giving 'strength' to the tree. The trunk and branches also contain nutrient storage cells, called parenchyma. The outer layers, as in hardwoods, are of cambium, bast and bark.

One of the most important parts of the tree is the leaf. It is in the leaves that energy from the sun converts water and carbon dioxide into the substances that are needed for tree growth. Leaves on trees are of many different shapes and sizes, so you can usually identify what kind of tree it is by looking carefully at its leaves.

46

Trees and other plants that lose their leaves in autumn are called deciduous. Two examples are the oak and the beech. Trees that shed their leaves a few at a time, are known as evergreens. The leaves fall off throughout the year, so the tree always has a large number of leaves on and appears permanently green. Examples here are pine and holly.

HOW DO TREES REPRODUCE THEMSELVES?

Trees reproduce themselves by making seeds. These are then distributed by gravity, animals, water or wind, to a new site where they germinate and grow into a new tree.

The reproductive part of broad-leaved trees is the flower. Some trees, such as lime and wild cherry, have both male (stamen) and female (carpel) parts in the same flower. Many trees, such as the oak, hazel and beech, have male and female parts in different flowers, but on the same tree. Some species, such as holly, poplar and willow, produce flowers of one sex on one tree and flowers of the other sex on another tree.

The male parts of the flower make pollen, which is then transferred to the female flower by insects or by the wind. The pollen fertilizes the ovule in the female part of the flower. Trees and shrubs that are wind-pollinated usually have a simple type of flower called a catkin. Catkins make vast quantities of pollen, which is then blown about by the wind. If pollen is to be spread most effectively by wind, there should be little interference by leaves — because leaves would both slow down the wind and catch large amounts of pollen. So these trees usually produce catkins (and therefore pollen) early in the year — before the leaves open. Some wind-pollinated trees come into leaf late in the spring. This group includes oak, hazel, ash, wych-elm, alder and birch.

Other trees and woodland plants are pollinated by insects. They therefore have brightly coloured or scented flowers to attract them. Insects come in search of the sweet nectar which is sometimes stored at the base of the petals. In so doing they unwittingly pick up pollen from the male part of the flower and then carry it from one flower to another — thus pollinating the female part of another tree. Shrubs and small woodland plants are nearly all insect-pollinated.

Examples here are hawthorn, rowan, holly, privet, spindle, dogwood, wayfaring tree and guelder rose.

After the ovule has been fertilized by the pollen grain it grows rapidly into a seed. Many seeds are protected by a fruit.

Fruits containing seeds can be of many kinds. For instance the fruits of the horse-chestnut are green and spiky and contain the seed that we know as the conker; the fruit of the oak is the acorn and the cup holding it; the sycamore fruit, containing the seed, has a wing so that the wind can distribute it over greater distances; the seeds of pines and firs are found in cones.

Mistletoe, which grows on branches of other trees, is an interesting plant. It produces a berry with a sticky seed that is eaten by birds like the mistle thrush. When the bird has eaten the berry it has to rub the sticky seed off its bill. It often does this against the branch of a tree, and so the seed is transferred to a new branch where it may grow.

A yew seed is spread in a similar way but, as it is not sticky, it drops to the ground once the bird has rubbed it off its bill.

Examine as many types of seed as you can find, decide how they are spread and notice the way in which they are scattered beneath the tree.

HOW DOES WIND AFFECT TREE GROWTH?

Try to find an isolated wood in the path of the wind, for instance on an exposed hillside or by the sea. What do you notice about the outline of the wood? The side nearest the prevailing wind is often lower and the bigger trees are found on the side away from the wind, where they are protected by the other trees. Strong winds also affect isolated trees causing them to bend away from the wind. In the autumn strong winds will often cause the leaves to change colour more quickly on the side of the tree facing the wind.

THE LARGEST TREES IN BRITAIN

The Newland Oak in the Forest of Dean in Gloucestershire measures 13·5 metres round the trunk — the greatest girth recorded for any British tree. Another large tree is a yew tree at Aldworth in Berkshire. It is thought by some to have stood for well over a thousand years! Its circumference 1·25 metres up from the ground is 8·2 metres.

The tallest tree in Britain is thought to be a Douglas fir at Powys Castle, Welshpool, which has grown to over 55 metres.

WHAT IS THE DIFFERENCE BETWEEN NATIVE AND INTRODUCED TREES?

Several thousand years ago Britain was joined to Europe by a narrow 'bridge' of dry land that crossed the English Channel from Kent to France. During this period much of the Arctic had a greater thickness of ice than it has today. As the climate became generally warmer most of this ice melted and the sea level rose. The sea flooded over the 'land bridge' and Britain was cut off from Europe and became an island. Only thirty-five species of trees in Britain today came naturally across this land bridge. These species are called native trees and are mainly hardwoods with broad leaves (for example the birch, alder, willow, hazel, oak and ash). There are three non-broad-leaved native species: the Scots pine, yew and juniper.

When the Romans came to Britain they brought seeds from the sweet chestnut. Because the climatic conditions and the soils in Britain suited it, the sweet chestnut survived and eventually spread its seeds throughout much of the land. It therefore belongs to the group of introduced trees.

Many other trees have been introduced including such well-known examples as the sycamore and horse chestnut. The Romans probably introduced the sycamore but the horse chestnut was brought to Britain much later, probably in the sixteenth or seventeenth century. Trees such as Sitka spruce and Douglas fir were introduced into Britain in the 1830s to produce quick-growing timber.

After the First World War the government introduced more quick-growing species because it was essential that we should be able to produce our own timber in time of war.

6
IDENTIFYING TREES

The shape, colour and arrangement of leaves, twigs, buds, bark and fruits give each tree its characteristics and hence its special name. When you are identifying trees it is a good idea to look for the various features in a regular or systematic order.

THE SHAPES OF SOME TREES IN WINTER

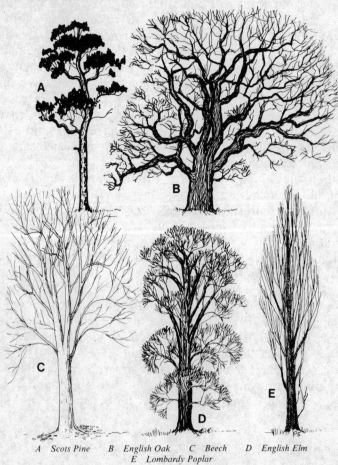

A   *Scots Pine*   B   *English Oak*   C   *Beech*   D   *English Elm*
E   *Lombardy Poplar*

With deciduous trees, the features you look for will vary depending on the season: in spring the buds are out; in summer the leaves are fully expanded; in autumn the fruits are on the tree; and in winter the shape of the tree is clearest. Whenever you can, try to find a branch of average size and age, as young twigs or old and withered branches may not have typical features (for books on tree identification, see page 121).

Look first at the general shape of the tree. A good time to start looking is in winter. It is perhaps easiest to select trees growing by themselves on parkland, hedgerows, roadside verges or in the middle of fields — you will be able to see the general shape or pattern of the tree more clearly when it is in an isolated position. Trees will vary with age, size, exposure to wind, the height above sea level at which they are growing, the type of soil, the slope on which they are situated and the amount of rainfall. Try to work out whether the tree has been influenced by any of these factors.

Look at the shape of the main trunk and the general arrangements of the branches. Some trees, such as Lombardy poplar, are tall and thin, with side branches growing in an upward direction. Wych elm has a large domed crown and spreading branches. An isolated holm oak may be almost square in its appearance, with its dark green leaves extending nearly to the ground. Birch is light and airy, while holly is dark and compact. Alder and hazel are short and bushy and beech can be tall and handsome.

The next feature to look at is the bark. Some barks are smooth, others rough; many have a characteristic colour — the silver-white of birch, the silver-grey of beech, the grey-brown of field maple, the pale grey of ash and the greenish-grey of holly. Barks can be difficult to identify as they can change a great deal from one part of the tree to another and can vary with the age and size of the branch or twig.

DECIDUOUS TREES
Buds and twigs
The best time to look at buds and twigs is in winter. The arrangement of buds on the twig is one of the most consis-

tent features of each tree species. Not only are they similar throughout each individual tree, but trees of the same species will have buds arranged in a similar pattern. At the end of each twig is a terminal bud, while lateral buds are found on the sides of the twig. Are the buds arranged in pairs along the stem or do they alternate? What colour are they? For example the ash has very distinctive black buds, while the horse-chestnut has bright brown sticky buds. What shape are the buds? Are they pointed like the beech, round like the hazel, stalked like the alder or rounded like the

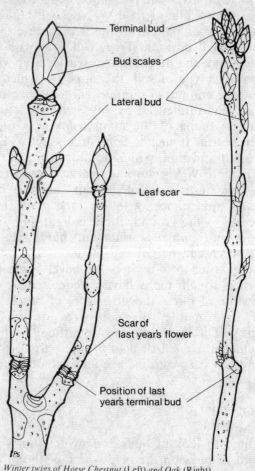

Terminal bud

Bud scales

Lateral bud

Leaf scar

Scar of
last year's flower

Position of last
year's terminal bud

Winter twigs of Horse Chestnut (Left) *and Oak* (Right)

lime? Are they large or small in comparison with the twig? Have they got many scales or only a few? Below each bud you will find a scar, which shows where a leaf was once joined to the stem. Note the pattern, shape and size of the scar.

Drawing twigs is an excellent way of noting their characteristics. Measure the sizes of the various parts with a pair of dividers and compare the actual size of your drawing. Always try to draw your twigs to scale. The relative sizes of the different parts of the twig and buds are often important for identification purposes. The size of the bud and the distance between buds may help you to distinguish one species from another.

Leaves
Leaves come in many different shapes, colours and sizes, so trees can usually be identified if you look carefully at their leaves. When examining and drawing leaves, ask yourself

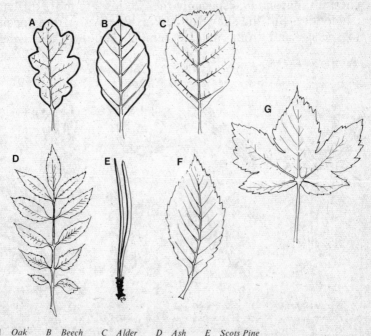

A Oak   B Beech   C Alder   D Ash   E Scots Pine
F Elm   G Sycamore

several questions. What is the shape of the leaf? Is it long and slender like the sweet chestnut, broad and round like the English elm or triangular like the poplar? Is the margin smooth like a walnut leaf, shaped and spiked like the holly, serrated like the sweet chestnut or does it have some other form? Do the leaves remain on the tree all the year round as they do on the holly, or do they fall in the autumn as they do on the ash? How are the veins arranged? Is there one simple leaf surface on each stem or is it compound — that is, split into many leaflets, like those of the rowan? Are the leaves lobed like the sycamore? Are the leaves stalked or stalkless? Are they hairy or non-hairy?

Flowers

Tree flowers, particularly the reduced or simple catkins, are sometimes difficult to identify unless you examine them with great care through a lens. There are, of course, some very characteristic flowers such as laburnum or horse-chestnut, but many, especially the catkins, are more difficult to identify. But the shape of catkins does vary from species to species and from male to female. Willow, oak, aspen,

FLOWERS OF TREES

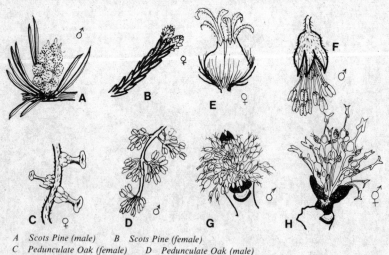

A   Scots Pine (male)   B   Scots Pine (female)
C   Pedunculate Oak (female)   D   Pedunculate Oak (male)
E   Beech (female)   F   Beech (male)   G   Ash (female)   H   Ash (male)

poplar and hazel are among many trees with catkins, while cherry, horse chestnut and blackthorn have 'typical' flowers with petals.

Fruits
The fruits of trees vary just as widely as the leaves and flowers. But there are a number of basic types and these will

SEEDS AND FRUITS OF TREES *(Not to scale)*

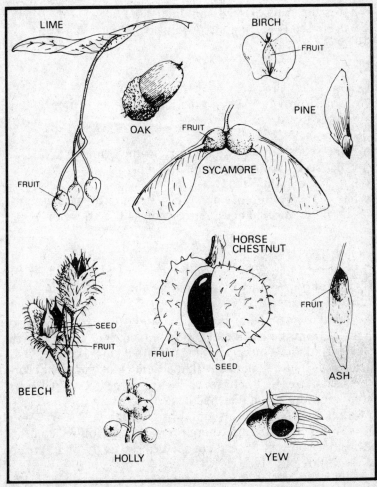

help you to identify the tree. When examining them, the questions you can ask are:

What time of year is the fruit shed?
Do fruits or seeds grow in groups or individually on the stalk?
What is the basic shape of the fruit?
Are the fruits juicy or dry?
Are they nutty, or like berries?
What is the fruit or seed container like?
Have the seeds got hairs or wings?
What size are they?

Seeds
Seeds also provide a key to the identification of trees. Some questions to ask are:

Are the seeds large and hard, or are they small?
Are the seeds borne in groups or singly?
What shape is the seed?
What is the colour of the seed? (Be careful here because seeds sometimes change their colour as they develop.)

CONIFERS

If you are identifying a conifer first try to place it in the right group or genus by examining the leaves. Then try to identify the species.

In order to find out the genus, study the arrangement of needles from the middle of a side branch. Ignore the upright shoots and the young seedlings, as they may not be characteristic. If the leaves are flattish and look more like tiny ferns your tree is likely to be a cypress or cedar. All other common conifers have 'needles'. Larches have clusters of needles on short shoots or nobs. Larches also lose their leaves in winter and are therefore called deciduous conifers. All other conifers have their needles set singly or in groups of two, three or five.

The hemlock is the easiest conifer with single needles to identify because its needles vary considerably in length. The yew has rather flattened needles and rather 'leafy' buds at the tip of the twigs.

Another group with single needles is spruce. Spruce needles are attached to the stem by a short peg. If you pull the needle away from the stem the peg usually comes as well. If you look at a spruce branch where the needles have fallen away naturally you will see rows of small pegs remaining. If there are no pegs then the tree is either a silver fir or a Douglas fir. The Douglas fir has oval, brown, slightly pointed papery buds at the tip of the branch, whereas the silver fir has a blunt, rounded bud. Junipers have spiky needles, set in groups of three round the stem, and have bluish berries. The last group is the pine, of which there are a large number. These have their needles arranged in groups of two, three or five.

Cones and seeds are usually characteristic. Compare them with the photographs or drawings in the identification books recommended on page 121

SOME FEATURES OF BROAD-LEAVED TREES AND CONIFERS

Broad-leaved trees	Feature	Conifers
net veined, usually deciduous (exceptions: holly, holm oak)	leaves	'needles', usually evergreen (exception: larch)
usually branching	trunk	usually straight to the top
hardwood	wood	softwood
no cones (exceptions: the alder has a type of cone)	seeds and fruits	woody cones (exceptions: juniper and yew)
usually little smell	buds and bark	often smell resinous
some wind-pollinated (catkins), others insect-pollinated (flowers)	flowers	always wind-pollinated (catkin-like)

7
WHAT IS A WOODLAND?

One interesting aspect of living in Britain is that the countryside changes rapidly from one region to another. For instance East Anglia looks completely different from the Downs of southern England, from the rugged mountains of the Lake District and from Snowdonia. Within each region there are also many variations. Norfolk, for example, has the Broads, heaths, sandy coasts, cliffs, coastal marshes, large areas of agricultural land and forests.

Woods, like the countryside, vary from place to place and from region to region. Next time you go on a long journey, take special note of the woods and trees. How do they differ from place to place?

Birch woodland—The Lake District

DOMINANT TREES

Climate and soil are two major features affecting trees. Wetter conditions are found in the more mountainous northern and western areas of Britain. Generally the upland areas of the north and west have poorer soils than the south and east. Not only is it generally colder in winter the further north and east you go in Britain, it also gets colder and wetter the higher you climb up a mountain.

Owing to changes in climate and soils, the dominant trees change from south to north, as do those from the bottom of the valley to the top of the mountain. In many places in the more mountainous parts of Britain you can see such changes quite clearly. In the Aber Valley in Gwynedd in North Wales, for instance, alders grow in profusion along the bottom of the valley, a mixture of elm and ash is found on the sides, while on the drier ground oak predominates. As you look up the side of the valley you can see that the oak and ash give way to birch, which in turn gives way to hawthorn. The trees become smaller and more stunted the higher up the hillside they grow, and they also become more scattered.

Where the soil and climatic conditions favour one kind of tree, this tree will usually grow in greater numbers and will soon become what is known as the dominant tree species. For instance if most of the trees in a wood are oak, then oak is said to be the dominant tree. Native woodlands in Britain are usually dominated by oak, ash, beech, pine or alder.

The most widespread type of hardwood or broad-leaved woodland found in Britain is oak woodland. This applies particularly to those parts of the country where there are fewest people, such as Dartmoor, or the Welsh valleys and hillsides.

If you live in southern or eastern Britain you will probably be familiar with beech woods. There are some particularly fine beech woods in the Chilterns, but others can be found in the New Forest, Epping Forest, in the Cotswolds and on the South Downs.

Oak tends to become dominant on heavier clay soils, whereas beech prefers the lighter chalky or limestone soils that are found largely in the central and south-eastern parts of Britain. This is obviously a broad generalization and you will often be able to find beech and oak growing within a few yards of one another.

Birch woods become extensive on poor or sandy soils and can often be found in conditions in which other trees will not grow. This is particularly true in the northern part of Britain, on high ground or on poor sandy soils. Because of their enormous number of light seeds which are easily blown great distances by wind, birch often colonize areas that have been cleared of other trees or plants. Because of their ability to live on poor soils they will often be the first colonizers of waste tips, slate heaps or mine-spoil tips. They are opportunists. There are two native species of birch: the silver birch, which is more common in the south; and the downy or hairy birch which, although present in southern England, is more common in the north and west. The main difference between the two is that the bark of silver birch develops large black diamonds on the white trunk. The leaves of the downy birch are more rounded and broadest in the middle, while the leaf of the silver is broadest near the base.

Scots pine forests are often found in similar situations to birch in southern England and in northern Scotland. Many sandy heaths contain scattered groups of Scots pine. In the Scottish Highlands this tree often forms large areas of forest.

The alder is a common tree throughout Britain. It grows in the wetter parts of woods made up chiefly of other trees, and small alder woodlands are also found along the wetter areas of many river valleys and in many upland bogs. It is particularly common in woodlands in Wales and western Scotland, whose wetter climates help to waterlog the soil. In Norfolk, particularly on the Norfolk Broads, there are many alder woods, which are known as carrs.

Of the remaining native trees one of the most interesting is the yew. Very few woods are dominated by yew, but it is frequently found on the chalky soil of southern England and on the South Downs in West Sussex and Hampshire. Some yews live a long time: many are known to be over five hundred years old, and some are thought to be nearly eight hundred years old.

Most of the other native British trees, such as hornbeam, holly, wych elm, rowan, lime, willow and poplar, rarely become dominant in a wood, but they are common in hedgerows and in small numbers within woodlands dominated by a wide range of other trees.

If we turn to the shrubs, hazel, hawthorn, blackthorn and gorse are all widely distributed. Juniper, although it does occur in many parts of Britain, is less common and, in wet areas, sallow is widespread.

ARE THERE ANY 'NATURAL' WOODS IN BRITAIN?

Woods on steep cliffs or in some of the very remote 'wilderness' areas of Scotland may be natural woodlands, as may woods on remote islands. In fact very few of Britain's offshore islands, particularly the remote ones, have trees on them at all because the high winds blowing off the sea cause conditions that trees do not like: strong, cool winds and salt spray, for example, prevent a young tree's shoots from developing properly.

Most woods of native species in Britain are more accurately called semi-natural woodlands, because man and his grazing animals have caused many changes within the woodland. Many plants that would occur naturally in a native woodland have been eaten by sheep and cattle and have long since disappeared. Clearing and replanting have altered the structure of many woods.

HOW CAN YOU RECOGNIZE MAN-MADE FORESTS?

You can recognize man-made forests quite easily because the trees within them are usually of similar age, are of only one or two species and are usually planted in rows. Man-made woods are often easily located on Ordnance Survey maps, as they frequently have rectangular boundaries.

In a wood that has not been touched by man or his grazing animals the trees will be of different ages. Some will have been killed off by lightning or disease thus leaving gaps in the forest. Young trees, not always of the same kind as those that have died, will grow in the space left by the dead trees. Very often birch trees will be the first trees to grow in a gap in a wood.

A man made forest — one or two species planted in rows

MAN-MADE FORESTS

One tree usually dominates man-made softwood forests. This is because the forester wishes to produce the most economic crop of trees. Just as the climate and the shape and nature of the ground determine which natural trees will become dominant, so they dictate to the forester which trees he should plant.

On Dartmoor, the Welsh Mountains, the Lake District and the western Highlands, for instance, the soils are usually acid, shallow and poorly drained. So when David Douglas was searching North America in the 1830s for trees to introduce into Britain, he chose the Sitka, because he found it growing naturally near the Pacific Coast in conditions that were not very different from those western upland parts of Britain. Although other trees will grow in these parts they need more shelter and a greater depth of soil than the Sitka. Sitka also grows well on the gentler hills of mid-Wales and the Scottish border country, although Norway spruce and Japanese larch also do well here.

As we move further east across Britain to areas where there is less rainfall and the mountains are less rugged, a wider variety of conifers flourish. Douglas fir, introduced to Britain by David Douglas, is perhaps the most suitable species, although larches also do well.

On the dry lands in eastern Scotland, north-eastern England, Norfolk and southern England, firs and pines are the main crop species.

DESCRIBING GROUPS OF TREES

Trees are usually described as a wood if large numbers of them are growing close together in a group. Of course the group can vary in size.

Here are some common terms for describing groups of trees:

Chase	a former royal forest that has gone into private ownership; Cannock Chase in Staffordshire was an example.
Clump	a group of trees less than 1/5 hectare; often planted as game cover
Compartment	part of a man-made forest, of about 10 hectares and usually bounded by forest roads and fire breaks.
Forest	if it is very large, it will be known as a forest, usually an ancient area such as the Forest of Dean, Sherwood Forest, New Forest, which probably originated from the royal hunting areas and in which the trees may be scattered. Large areas of modern or recent planting are also known as forests (for example the Gwydyr Forest in North Wales, the Grizedale Forest in the Lake District or the Thetford Forest in East Anglia).
Grove	a wood less than 2 hectares but larger than a clump.
Line	trees planted fairly close together in one or two rows, usually along the side of a road or drive.
Plantation	a woodland planted by man and usually made up of coniferous trees planted at the

	same time; a forest can be made up of several plantations.
Scrub	a term given to trees or bushes (such as hawthorn) that are stunted in growth; scrub is frequently found on the upper slopes of hills at altitudes above which larger trees will not grow; some woodlands that have been felled and are regenerating can be called scrub woodlands if the trees are under 7 metres in height.
Shelter belt	usually a strip several rows wide or a rectangular block of trees planted in order to provide shelter for animals.
Spinney	usually an area of dense shrub growth containing hawthorn and blackthorns, though it may contain other species as well.
Stand	any area of woodland in which all the trees are of one species.
Thicket	a dense growth of trees and vegetation, or a young plantation in which trees have not been thinned so that it is very difficult to penetrate the centre of the plantation.
Wood	an area of 2 hectares or more that is tree-covered and usually dominated by one or a few species of tree.

WOODLAND STRUCTURE

Just as different human families live on different floors of a block of flats, so different kinds of plants tend to be found on different levels or layers within the wood. Look for these layers in a wood or on a photograph or drawing. Sometimes there is bare soil under the trees, perhaps with a covering of dead leaves; then come mosses and small plants; elsewhere there will be grasses and flowering plants. These three lowest layers in a wood are referred to as follows — the soil; the ground layer (containing the mosses); and the herb layer (containing flowering plants).

Some woods have bushes of privet, hawthorn, blackthorn, or bramble. These make up what is known as the shrub layer. Above the shrub layer there are small trees, which

Woodland Structure
1 Ground Layer   2 Herb Layer   3 Under-Storey   4 Canopy (open)

may include rowan, hazel and alder. The branches and leaves of these trees fill in the space between the shrubs and the main leafy crown of the larger forest trees. This layer of smaller trees is called the under-storey. The highest level of all is the one formed by the tops of the largest trees, which covers the rest of the wood and is called the canopy.

To make simplified diagrams of the wood you wish to study, imagine a line along the edge, or through the middle of your wood. Draw the outline of the plants and trees that fall on your imaginary line (or transect). For practice make a simplified drawing from a photograph or picture that shows the layers of the wood. You will now have a diagram of the vertical structure of a wood.

Your drawing of a real wood will probably resemble one of the following: a wood in which all the layers are present; a wood in which some of the layers are missing; and a conifer plantation in which only large trees are present.

Many woods in which all the trees are beech, particularly where they grow close together, have no ground, herb or shrub layers and probably no under-storey. But if you look at the edge of the wood you may find some of the other layers present there; why, then, are they missing from the middle of the beech wood? To find out you will have to go into the wood. Pick a part where all the layers except the canopy are missing, look directly upwards and describe what you see. You will probably see layer upon layer of beech leaves. The canopy will be so dense that little sunlight will reach the ground. Such a thick canopy, forming a continuous cover, is called a closed canopy. As most plants need a good deal of light in order to grow, the thicker the closed canopy, the more likely it is that the lower layers of plants will be missing. If the canopy is not continuous — if you can see patches of sky where the leaves do not meet — it is said to be an open canopy. Under an open canopy most of the other layers will probably be present.

If most of a wood has a closed canopy, pay particular attention to the areas where there is a gap. Usually light floods into the wood through such gaps and you will find a mass of ground and shrub layer plants. Such areas are

Looking up at closed canopy woodland in winter

Looking up at open canopy woodland in winter

known as glades. Paths or 'rides' through woods resemble such areas, but often the under-storey and herb layers are missing, because many of the shrubs and herbs are trodden down by walkers, forest workers or animals.

Sometimes even where plenty of light comes through there are still very few plants. This lack of vegetation is usually caused by many farmers allowing their animals, particularly sheep, to wander into the wood for shade in summer and shelter from wind and rain in winter. These animals graze the young shoots of trees and other plants and they therefore do not grow.

But it is not only domestic animals that affect the shape of a wood in this way. Deer, for example, spend much of their time in forests and, as they are grazing animals, eat much of the vegetation in the lower woodland layers.

SOME FACTORS AFFECTING THE STRUCTURE OF A WOODLAND

animals	grazing animals (wild and domestic)
	seed-eating animals
	wood-boring insects
climate	frost
	humidity
	rain
	snow
	temperature and sunlight
	wind
disease	diseases of trees
	virus
man	wood required for building
	„ „ for fuel
	„ „ for furniture
	„ „ for paper
	„ „ for tanning
other plants	dense growth of some plants, preventing seedlings from growing
	fungi causing timber to rot
rocks	depth under the soil
	type of rock
soil	depth of soil,
	drainage
	type of soil (peaty, sandy, clay)

8
LIVES OF WOODLAND PLANTS

Many of our best-known and most-loved wild flowers, such as the bluebell, daffodil, lily-of-the-valley, wood anemone, honeysuckle, primrose and cuckoo-pint, are woodland plants. But there are so many different kinds of woodland plants that it would be impossible to describe them all in this book. Luckily there are many good plant identification books on the market and you will find a list of some of them on page 121. If you are making your first woodland study, list some of the plants you are likely to find in the various types of wood in your district. By the side of each name note the month in which the plant flowers, then go and look for it.

Study the different parts of woodland plants. What are the roots like? Are they fibrous roots like grasses or tap roots like dandelions? How deep in the soil do the roots penetrate? Do the roots make use of the different layers of soil?

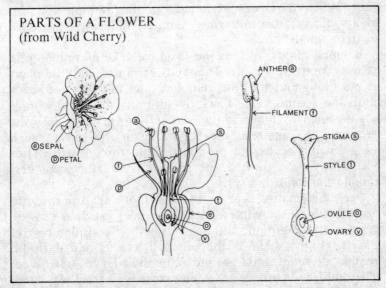

PARTS OF A FLOWER
(from Wild Cherry)

ⓔSEPAL
ⓓPETAL

ANTHERⓐ
FILAMENTⓕ
STIGMAⓢ
STYLEⓣ
OVULEⓞ
OVARYⓥ

Do the plants have underground food-storage organs such as the bulbs of bluebells and snowdrops or the corms of the cuckoo-pint? With a little careful fieldwork you should be able to answer these and many other questions. Look at the stems and leaves and ask yourself how are they arranged? How are they placed within the wood? And how do they compete with other plants?

LIFE CYCLE OF A PLANT

The life of each plant follows a definite pattern, which is known as its life cycle. Life cycles vary widely but in its simplest form the term refers to the way in which young plants are produced, pass through a number of stages to maturity and eventually reproduce more young. Some flowering plants take a year to complete the life cycle, others take two years. Most trees do not produce seeds (the starting-point of a new cycle) for several years.

Annual plants pass through the winter as seeds only. In spring the seeds germinate, grow into plants, produce flowers and then seeds. After forming seeds the plant dies, leaving the seeds to continue the cycle in the following year. When the seeds germinate in the autumn and the plants die off the following summer, they are known as winter annuals.

Biennial plants, such as the foxglove, take more than one year to complete a cycle. The seeds germinate and the plant grows thoughout the first year but does not produce seeds until the second year. Towards autumn large food-storage organs such as tubers grow and it is from these that the growth starts again at the beginning of the second year. Flowers and seeds are produced from this growth. After seeds have been formed, the plant dies and the seeds germinate the following spring.

Perennial plants, such as the coltsfoot and primrose, do not die during the winter. Some perennials, such as grasses, remain above ground, although growth is considerably reduced. Others, such as the bluebell, crocus and daffodil, remain dormant underground once their leaves have died. The bulbs and corms or rhizomes store food from which the plants will burst forth the following spring.

FLOWERING SEASONS

Some botanists divide the year up into five flowering seasons. These flowering seasons are related to the leaf stages of the wood: the pre-leaf flowering stage (pre-vernal); the early leaf flowering stage (vernal); the summer flowering stage (aestival); the autumn flowering stage (autumnal); and lastly the winter stage (hiemal). The timing of these stages varies from the north to the south of Britain, and often from the east to the west. In an average season the stages might run from the end of February to the end of April; from May to mid-June; from mid-June to early September; from mid-September to November; and from December to the end of February.

Here are some examples:

pre-vernal flowers	primroses and dog's mercury
vernal	bluebells and oak
aestival	twayblades and willow herb
autumnal	no woodland flowers (although some aestival flowers may extend into this stage)
hiemal	hazel

Dog's Mercury

Bird's-nest Orchid

A woodland floor in the pre-vernal stage

Rose Hips — the fruits of Wild Rose

CHARTING WOODLAND FLOWERS

Whenever you observe a wild flower in a wood note the month and enter it on to a bar chart. If you make two bar charts in successive years, you will be able to look for differences owing to early or late springs, hot or cool summers, dry or wet autumns.

From books you will be able to find the average flowering seasons throughout Britain. You will then be able to compare your chart with the national picture and see whether the flowers in your district come into the early, mid or late part of the season. Below is an example of a bar chart showing flowering seasons.

You could also make a bar chart showing the flowering periods of the trees.

BAR CHART SHOWING FLOWERING SEASONS

MONTHS

Flower	J	F	M	A	M	J	J	A	S	O	N	D
Winter aconite	■	■										
Mezereon		■	■									
Dog's mercury	■	■	■									
Spurge laurel			■	■								
Barren strawberry		■	■	■	■	■						
Primrose		■	■	■	■							
Wood anemone			■	■	■							
Green hellebore			■	■								
Lesser celandine			■	■	■	■						
Wood spurge			■	■	■							
Moschatel				■	■							
Cuckoo-pint				■	■							
Woodland violet	■	■	■	■	■							
Wood sorrel				■	■							
Common violet			■	■	■							
Bluebell				■	■							
Wild strawberry				■	■	■						
Goldilocks				■	■							
Lily-of-the-valley					■	■						
Sweet woodruff					■	■						
Bugle					■	■	■					
Columbine					■	■	■					
Herb paris					■	■	■					
Wood forget-me-not					■	■	■					
Yellow dead nettle					■	■	■					
Sanicle					■	■	■					
Bird's nest orchid				■	■	■						
Chickweed wintergreen						■	■					
Yellow bird's nest						■	■					
Woody nightshade						■	■					
Goosegrass						■	■					
Marsh thistle						■	■	■				
Honeysuckle						■	■	■				
Enchanter's nightshade						■	■					
Mountain St John's wort						■	■					
Greater bell-flower						■	■					
Melancholy thistle						■	■	■				
Foxglove						■	■	■				
Golden rod						■	■	■				
Wood sage						■	■	■				

WHEN DO FLOWERING PLANTS PRODUCE THEIR LEAVES?

Leaves use the sun's energy to make the food materials the plants need. So the period of the year when there is the greatest amount of leaf is important to the plant.

We can trace the stages when plants are most active in producing food materials through their leaves. These stages are: before the main tree canopy leaves are formed (pre-vernal); summer green leaves; those that form new leaves in the autumn which remain through the winter; and lastly the evergreens. Examples of these are:

pre-vernal species	bluebell, lesser celandine, wood anemone, goldilocks, cuckoo-pint and spotted orchid
summer green	honeysuckle, woodruff, enchanter's nightshade and dog's mercury
wintergreen	primrose, bugle, wood spurge and archangel
evergreen	ivy

You can add to this list from your own observations, and then make a bar chart similar to the one for the flowering periods.

HOW DO WOODLAND FLOWERING PLANTS RE-PRODUCE THEMSELVES?

Woodland flowering plants reproduce their kind either by producing seeds or by a process of vegetative growth. In order to produce seeds the female part of the plant must be pollinated. Many trees and a few woodland plants are wind-pollinated. Other trees and woodland plants are pollinated by insects that visit the flowers in search of nectar. They then pick up some pollen and carry it from one flower to another, thus pollinating the latter.

Many plants pollinated by moths have light-coloured or white flowers. This is probably to make them more obvious to moths, most of which fly at dusk or at night. Other moth-pollinated flowers, such as the honeysuckle and butterfly orchid, have strong scents so as to attract night-flying insects.

Relatively few herb-layer plants are wind-pollinated, because vegetation would seriously hinder the dispersal of pollen by the wind. One exception is dog's mercury, which produces flowers, and therefore pollen, very early in the year. Once the ovule has been fertilized by pollen the seed begins to develop.

Seeds are produced in many shapes and sizes and are dispersed in many different ways. Many seeds fall from the plant. Some of these are taken by birds or animals for food, but many are simply dropped on to the ground. The cuckoo-pint is an example of a plant with edible seeds — the bird or animal often breaks into the plant to obtain the seed.

The seed containers of plants such as the violet, vetch, broom and gorse dry out and set up a tension that splits the case, thus flicking out the seeds. Orchids rely on wind to distribute their tiny seeds. Wind is also used to disperse the seeds of those plants that produce seeds attached to 'parachutes'. Dandelions, thistles and willow herb all come into this group.

The white campion and Welsh poppy have an unusually long flower stalk. The seed container turns into a dry capsule containing a number of seeds and at the top of this is a ring of holes. When the wind blows the flower stalk waves from side to side, shaking the seeds out of the capsule. Next time you come across a poppy a few weeks after the petals have fallen, look out for this.

Several plants, including goosegrass, burdock and woodruff, have hooked seeds that cling to the hairs of passing animals and later fall off, often some distance away from the parent plant.

Plants don't always reproduce themselves by the process of pollination — fertilization — seed production — germination. Many herbaceous flowering plants reproduce their numbers by vegetative growth for most of the time. They do this either below ground by means of specially developed types of roots or above ground by means of runners. The wood anemone is an example of the former and the wild strawberry an example of the latter.

BULBS AND CORMS

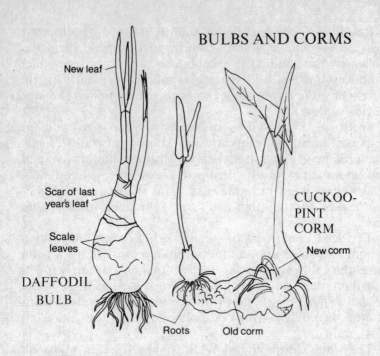

New leaf

Scar of last
year's leaf

Scale
leaves

DAFFODIL
BULB

CUCKOO-
PINT
CORM

New corm

Roots   Old corm

LOOKING FOR WOODLAND FLOWERS

Very few flowering plants are found in only one type of
woodland. The type of soil and the amount of light passing
through the leaves are usually more important than the type
of woodland in determining the variety of plants you will
find there. For example, man-planted conifer woods are
usually very dark, with a thick layer of 'needles' covering the
ground — there are few or no plants on the ground or herb
layers. Beech woods are often well shaded because of their
dense canopy while oak woods are more sunny but not as
sunny as ash woodlands. Birch woods are often the most
open and lightest of all.

Certain plants prefer specific parts of woods — for
example, many flowers are found only at the edge of the
wood or in boundary hedges. The woodland violet and the
common violet are both found along woodland rides, glades
or on the edge of the wood. The enchanter's nightshade also
likes rides and glades. Betony, greater stitchwort, bindweed,
woody nightshade, greater bell-flower and goosegrass all

Man-planted conifer woods are usually yery dark

like hedgerows. Dog's mercury, bluebell, wood sorrel, wood anemone and sanicle can be found scattered thoughout many woods. Foxgloves and greater bell-flowers like woodland clearings, though the latter are also found in hedges.

When looking for woodland flowers you will have to choose your wood carefully. If it has been heavily grazed by sheep or cattle most of the flowering herbs will have disappeared and grasses will be the dominant plants in the herb layer. In upland oak, birch and pine woods, common bent grass, the velvet bent, scented vernal grass ·and the wavy hair grass will ·be the most usual species. On the dryer, richer soils, wood melick and wood falsebrome are common and ·species such as wood barley, woodland brome, wood and giant fescue are found. In wetter, grazed woodlands a number of species of rush, sedge and grass, such as purple moor grass, are common. If the woods are fenced to keep cattle and sheep out, a much wider variety of flowering plants will be found.

BIRCH WOODS

Birch woods are among the lightest and most open in structure. Birch is a pioneer species often growing on poor soils and colonizing waste tips of coal mines, slate quarries or other stone and ore workings. Birch is rarely found on chalk but will grow on most other types of soil. It is common on sandy heaths, limestones, acid raised bogs and alkaline fens. Because birch trees grow on so many different types of soil in many parts of the country, you will find a wide variety of plants in birch woods. However, because birch woods often grow on poor soils, each individual wood may have only a small number of different plants in it.

PINE WOODS

The Scots pine is another pioneer species that grows on a wide range of soil types. Because both birch and pine grow in similar situations, the plants that grow in them are often similar. Such plants as heather, bilberry and tormentil are common. Compare your plant lists of pine woods with those of birch woods in similar situations.

If pine or birch woods are next to heathy areas then heather, bilberry or bracken may still form thick carpets under the trees. In many Scottish pine forests, juniper grows under the dominant trees. But if pines are growing close together, then the deep shade will eliminate many of the other woodland plants.

Because many of the soils found in the uplands of Scotland and the North of England are acid peats there are only a few species of flower found in many native pine forests. One, the unusually named chickweed wintergreen, is related neither to chickweeds nor to wintergreens. It is a member of the primrose family and has a whorl or ring of leaves near the top of the stem and a delicate white starry flower. The wintergreens are the other group of flowers that you may be lucky enough to come across in pine woods.

ASH WOODS

Ash woods are often mixed in with other trees or found in hedgerows. In the limestone areas of the North of England you may come across woods that contain almost exclusively ash trees. Ash woods are usually light sunny places. This is due to the rather widespread arrangement of the branches and to the very broken or divided shape of the leaves, which allow plenty of sunlight to pass through. So you will probably find more summer flowering plants in ash woods than in woods with thick closed canopies. Such plants as the lily-of-the-valley, bloody cranesbill and mountain St John's wort are found in some of the dryer ash woods, while on wetter soils wild garlic often forms thick carpets of white flowers and bright green leaves. The yellow dead nettle, sometimes called the yellow archangel, and not related to the stinging nettle, is often found in ash woods. And so are two thistles — the marsh thistle and the melancholy thistle.

OAK WOODS

In oak woods — if the soils are fairly dry, that is, on a good freely draining slope — you will often find a lot of bracken, in which there will be bluebells, wood sage and foxgloves. In the under-storey in oak woods you will frequently find hazels on wetter soils and on very wet soils, small alders and willows.

Some early common flowers of oak woods are the lesser celandine, dog's mercury, wood anemone and primrose. A little later bluebells appear together with ground ivy, common and woodland violets, wood spurge, green hellebore and stinking hellebore. As spring passes into summer the little moschatel may be found. Woodland buttercup, goldilocks and, in many parts of the country, wood forget-me-not, will flower under the oak wood's early summer canopy. By June it is the turn of bugle, enchanter's nightshade, columbine and herb paris. Two other oak woodland flowers are the golden rod and the wood sage, while on poorer soils the great wood-rush, bilberry and honeysuckle are common.

BEECH WOODS

Several of the flowers of the oak wood will also be found in beech woods. Beech woods, with their many layers of spreading branches and round leaves, often cut out more sunlight than oak woods and as a result there is very often less plant life under beeches than under the oak. In many beech woods nothing grows under the trees because, in addition to the small amount of sunlight, the ground is covered by a deep layer of dead leaves. When beeches are spread out then you will frequently find wood sorrel, dog's mercury, hairy violet and perhaps patches of bramble within the wood.

Two unusual plants are found in beech woods: the yellow bird's nest and the bird's nest orchid. Both these plants flower in June and July when the woods allow very little sunlight to pass through the leaf canopy. These plants are unusual because they do not use sunlight to make food in the leaves. They rely on fungi to make their food for them from decaying leaves that cover the ground. You may be lucky enough to find several orchids in beech woods. Some of the helleborines, particularly the white helleborine, are also beech wood species.

At the edges of the beech wood, where more sunlight is able to reach the ground layer and where wind can blow away some of the dead leaves that would otherwise cover the soil, you should find several more herbaceous flowering plants and grasses. Dog's mercury, ivy and wood sanicle are some of these. You may also find an interesting little shrubby plant, the evergreen spurge laurel, with its clusters of greenish flowers or black fruits. A close relative of the spurge laurel, also found in some beech woods, is the mezereon, which is not evergreen and has pale reddish-purple flowers and scarlet fruits.

The wild strawberry grows in some of the more open beech woods, where its runners can sometimes be found in great abundance on grassy banks and woodland edges. The sweet woodruff, with its rings of pointed leaves round the stem and cluster of white funnel-shaped flowers, will frequently be found in May or June.

Of course you will come across many other flowers on your woodland walks and you will also find flowers growing where you don't expect to find them for many flowers grow in several different kinds of woodland. By continually noting the plants you find and by asking questions about them and the wood itself, you will begin to see some patterns emerging and will find that the vegetation of several woods with one really dominant tree species will have similar groups of plants which differ from those with other dominant trees.

9
FLOWERLESS PLANTS IN WOODS

Hundreds of different and fascinating flowerless plants are to be seen in woods — fungi, mosses, liverworts, lichens, algae and ferns.

Most flowering plants grow on the ground, although a few, such as mistletoe, grow on trees. But flowerless plants grow in a wider variety of places. Fungi are found growing on branches and trunks of living and dead trees, on fallen leaves in the soil and on roots of trees. Some flowerless plants are associated with many different types of trees or woodland, while others are found only in one kind of wood or on one kind of tree.

There are too many different kinds of flowerless plant for me to describe or even name them all in one chapter. You will need to get one of the field guides or specialist books on flowerless plants to help you (see the list on page 121).

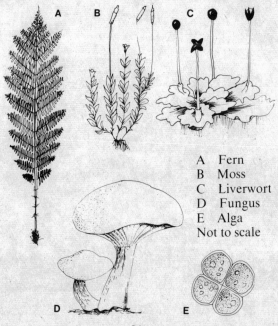

A   Fern
B   Moss
C   Liverwort
D   Fungus
E   Alga
Not to scale

FUNGI

There are many kinds of fungi: bracket fungi found growing on trunks and branches of trees; mushrooms and toadstools on the woodland floor or on rotting timber; and moulds, which are usually found in damp or humid parts of the wood.

The hypha is the basic part of a fungus. Many hyphae form a mycelium that spreads out over the food substance, often forming a filmy structure. The familiar mushroom or toadstool is a packed collection of hyphae that form the fungal fruiting body. Fungi do not depend directly upon the sun for food, as flowering plants do. Instead they take organic matter from other plants or animals. Fungi can be parasitic (living off the tissues of a living organism) or saprophitic (living off dead plant and animal material and causing further decay).

A Woodland Gill Fungus

Fungi reproduce both sexually and asexually. Sexual reproduction involves the fusion of fungal nuclei in special hyphae. In asexual reproduction, millions of microscopic spores are produced and scattered into the air. If they drift on to a suitable substratum they will grow into new hyphae.

Moulds are collections of hyphae on which a number of spore bodies can develop. Mushrooms have a mycelium from which a 'fruiting body' is formed. The fruit body often consists of a stalk with a cap. On the underside of the cap are radiating gills on which the spores are produced. There are many variations and you will require a special book on fungi which will describe these. The best time to look for fungi is in the autumn, from September to early December, for this is the time when most fruit bodies appear.

A Bracket Fungus on a Birch trunk

Puffballs — ground layer Fungi

FUNGI IN PINE WOODS

Two fungi found in conifer woods are the pine-wood mushroom and the false chanterelle. Other species are some of the milkcaps (the liver milkcap and the red milkcap) and many of the small delicate 'bonnet' fungi belonging to the mycena family.

All the fungi we have talked about so far have gills, as do the mushrooms we eat. But other forms of mushrooms have tubes in place of gills. If you look under the cap of one of the boletus species you will see the ends of a large number of these tubes — they look like a lot of small holes in the fleshy part of the fungus. Several of the boletus species grow in conifer woods. Several cup fungi are also found under conifers.

One of the most spectacular of our fungi is the fly agaric. This bright red-and-white capped fungus is often illustrated because of its spectacular appearance. It is found in pine and birch woods. The fly agaric is poisonous and was once often made into fly killers.

FUNGI IN BEECH WOODS

Perhaps the most poisonous of our fungi is a species closely related to the fly agaric, the death cap fungus, which is frequently found in beech woods.

The horn of plenty and the chanterelle are also found in beech woods, though they do occur in other woodlands as well. One very distinctive beech wood fungus is the beech tuft, a shining white, sticky fungus that grows in clumps on trunks, or branches.

FUNGI IN OAK WOODS

Many fungi are to be found in oak woods and the beef steak fungus, a bracket fungus, is one of the most distinctive of these. The bracket fungi grow on trunks or branches of trees and live off either the sap wood or the heart wood. Some will attack living trees, while others prefer dead wood.

Many fungi of deciduous woodlands are found in oak woods but several, like *Russula vesca, Cortinarius hinnuleus* and *Collybia dryophila* are particularly common.

One of the more interesting aspects of looking for fungi is the great variety of shapes, size and colour you will find. The bright purple of the blewits, the red of *Russula emetica* and the lemon-yellow of *Russula violeipes;* the white and black inkcaps, the black rounded King Alfred's cakes or the fleshy ear fungus; the cup fungi with their bright orange, red or yellow interiors; the stinkhorns and the puffballs — all these add up to a most fascinating group of flowerless plants.

ALGAE

The algae are a large primitive group of plants. They have a simple structure compared with flowering plants. Many have only one, two or four cells or form a chain of similar cells. The larger algae cannot be divided into root and shoot and they do not have well-defined conducting vessels for carrying food substances.

Algae such as sea lettuce, kelp and wrack are common on our coast lines. But few conspicuous large algae are found in woods. Perhaps the most familiar is the green covering found on the barks of many trees. This green 'dust' is a small single-celled green alga that grows in large numbers on the rain tracks of tree trunks. Next time you go into a wood, see if you can see this alga and note where it grows. Does it grow on all sides of the trunk or is it more abundant on one side? If it is more abundant on one side, which side is this and why? You should be able to work that one out for yourself!

LICHENS

The lichens are another large group of interesting plants — with some features of the fungi and some of the algae. Some of the woodland lichens are upright and branched while others form flat, dry-looking discs or crusts on tree trunks or branches. You can look for lichens on rocks, or on walls in the wood, while some species grow on the ground. Although you may be able to identify some of the more spectacular lichens from the illustrations in books, you would be well advised to try to obtain help from a biologist or a museum.

MOSSES AND LIVERWORTS

The mosses and liverworts are yet another group of plants that require great care and attention in their identification. The liverworts and mosses are called bryophytes by botanists. The bryophytes are mostly fairly small plants, the largest rarely growing to a height of more than 25 centimetres and the majority are much smaller. In spite of their size they are plants of great beauty, especially when viewed in their natural habitat and through a lens. Many mosses,

Moss capsules

especially in the damper parts of western Britain, form thick carpets on woodland floors. There are about 300 kinds of liverwort and 600 mosses in Britain.

You will find it difficult to identify many species, but it is still worthwhile trying to sort out one or two of the more distinctive ones. Obtain advice if you can. A pocket lens is a great help. Even if you can't identify species you will get great enjoyment from a close examination of the plants — with their delicate colouring and shape and the great variety of 'fruiting bodies' or spore-producing capsules.

Mosses consist of stems, with a distinct strand in the centre, and of leaves and rhizoids (tiny root-like cells). Liverworts are found mainly in damp places. In the simpler liverworts the plant body is a flat greenish structure, called a thallus, which has a number of rhizoids, larger than those of mosses, growing from the underside.

CLUBMOSSES, HORSETAILS AND FERNS

The last major group of flowerless plants are the clubmosses, horsetails and ferns. Unlike clubmosses, horsetails and ferns are often found in woods. The twenty or so species of horsetails found on earth today are the sole surviving members of a much larger group that flourished 250 million years ago. In the Carboniferous coal-forming forests of former geological times horsetails frequently grew to the size of trees, but today they are much smaller. They can easily be recognized by the jointed stem with rings of tooth-like leaves that join to form a circular sheath at the joints.

Ferns have a lot of leaf, called fronds, and little stem. Ferns like moist, damp woodlands with damp humus-type soils. So don't be surprised to find a great abundance of ferns in many woodlands in the wetter, more mountainous western parts of Britain. In many woods ferns grow in such numbers that they can be seen growing from branches and trunks of trees. Plants that grow on trees in this way are called epiphytes.

Some of the common woodland ferns to look for are lady fern, buckler fern, prickly shield, hard fern, polypody, bracken and male fern.

10
LARGER ANIMALS IN WOODS

A large number of British animals spend all or some of their time in woodlands — hardly surprising when we consider that most of Britain was originally covered by trees before man burnt and felled them. Animals live in all parts of the wood, ranging from under the ground to the canopy, and of course they move from place to place.

What do we mean when we say animals? As well as the large mammals such as badgers, foxes, deer or rabbits biologists include other animals with backbones (called vertebrates), such as fish; amphibians, like the toad and frog; reptiles, like the snakes and lizards; and birds. A large number of animals have no backbones (invertebrates). This group includes woodlice, centipedes, many kinds of insects, spiders and snails.

WHAT DO ANIMALS USE WOODS FOR?
Many animals obtain all their living requirements from woods: food, cover from predators, nest or home sites in which to bring up their young, sites for shelter and places in which to hibernate. For animals that hibernate, woods provide a plentiful supply of dead leaves that are gathered for bedding material and are used to keep the sleeping animal warm throughout the winter. Hedgehogs, bats and dormice hibernate in this way. Some animals will use the woodland for sleeping or bringing up their young but will hunt for food over large areas of neighbouring land.

LARGER ANIMALS FOUND IN WOODS
Many people think of red and grey squirrels as the most typical woodland animals because they are about in daylight and can be seen springing from tree to tree.

The native roe, fallow and red deer are frequently found in forests, though they do feed on surrounding grasslands and moorlands as well. Several species of deer that have been introduced into Britain are also found mainly in woodlands.

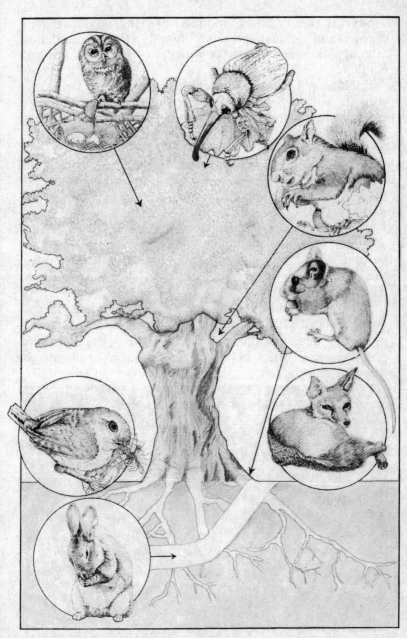

Animals live in all parts of the wood

Several of our rarer animals, like the wild cat, pine marten and polecat, are also animals of the woodlands, although they are mainly confined to parts of Wales and Scotland.

Rabbits, and to a lesser extent brown hares, are frequently seen in woods. Several different kinds of bat have been recorded in our forests — particularly if there are a number of dead trees with large holes in which they can sleep and hibernate.

In southern England, particularly in beech woods, the dormouse is still found, but as this animal is nocturnal, hibernates and is thought to be decreasing in number, it is not seen very often. The majority of the other small mammals, like shrews, moles, bank voles and woodmice, are very common in most woodlands. Sometimes their populations become very large and the mammals that prey on them, such as stoats, weasels and foxes, will also become abundant.

Just as man introduced many tree species into Britain so he introduced several animals and birds. Apart from Chinese water deer, muntjak and sika deer, the edible dormouse, grey sqirrel and little owl have been introduced within the last hundred years or so.

Weasel

Rabbit

Shrew

91

Wood mice

REPTILES AND AMPHIBIA
If there are wet areas in your woodland you may come across some amphibia (frogs, toads and newts). In a heathy woodland lizards or adders are found while in other woodlands grass snakes or other reptiles are quite common. (For identification books, see list on page 121.)

BIRDS AND WOODS
Birds make use of every part of the woodland in every part of Britain. Every layer of the wood is used for feeding and for nesting, although some species have distinct preferences: blue tits and coal tits like the canopy and the small twigs; the marsh tit prefers lower, larger branches; and the great tit frequently searches for food in the lower levels or on the ground. Start making notes on where and in which types of tree you see each species.

Nest sites are found in every situation: herons, rooks and magpies nest high up in the canopy: crows and mistle thrushes use a forked branch high in the tree; woodpeckers make their own holes for their nests in the trunk or branches while tits, starlings, pied flycatchers, redstarts and owls use natural holes; treecreepers nest behind bark where this has started to come away from the bast; robins, dunnocks, thrushes and blackbirds hide their nests in shrubs; and willow warblers, wood warblers and chiffchaffs use dense ground vegetation.

Woods give protection from predators, although birds like the sparrowhawk have developed superb flying techniques and manoeuvrability and are frequently able to surprise smaller prey.

HOW TO FIND LARGER ANIMALS IN WOODS
There are many different ways of setting out to look for animals and the animals you find will depend on the method you choose.

Perhaps one of the most exciting ways of discovering the habits of woodland animals is to go into a wood at night with an experienced zoologist. The best time for seeing many nocturnal animals, like the badger, fox and wood mouse, is at dusk or at first light when they are hurrying back to their homes. I have often stood absolutely still by a

Hazel nuts eaten by Wood Mice

tree in the early morning, before the sun has risen to its full height, and watched a fox returning to its lair.

One essential part of animal watching is to keep still and quiet. If you sit by a wall or tree stump you may see wood mice, stoats, weasels or a host of other mammals as they search for food.

The early morning watch has many advantages: not only are you likely to see the last of the nocturnal hunters returning to their dens but also there is usually great activity as the first daylight hunters stir from their sleep. Squirrels are particularly active at this time of day and you will often see them running along the ground searching for fallen nuts.

Many larger woodland animals, particularly deer and foxes, have a keen sense of smell. If you are tracking animals, always remember to let the wind blow from the animal towards you and not the other way round.

In many cases a hide will be useful, especially when you know where animals' paths, sets or earths are. Several Forestry Commission forests, such as Grizedale in the Lake District, have observation platforms from which you can watch deer, other animals and birds.

Some animals are very difficult to catch sight of but are easy to trace. For example, mole hills and tunnels can be clearly seen on the surface of the ground.

Another rewarding pastime is looking for, identifying and following animal tracks. You can track animals by their footprints in daytime and obtain a number of clues as to where to look for the animals that made them. This is time-saving, particularly when the animals are night hunters. You may enjoy making plaster casts of animals' footprints. To do this you need a mixing tin, some plaster of Paris and a bottle of water. Find a good clear foot print, mix your plaster and water into a firm paste, place the mixture in the foot print, allow to dry, carefully lift out and, with a bit of luck, you will have a good cast.

11
BIRDS IN WOODS

Birds are relatively easy to study, because not only are most of them about in daylight, but they are also reasonably large animals, often with distinctive colours, shapes, habits and songs. Learn to make careful notes when observing birds. First note any distinctive feature or colour, then try to describe the plumage systematically. Eye stripes, crown, nape, back, rump, cheek, flank and belly colours; tail, particularly if there are distinctive outer or central feathers, and wings should then be described. Bill, legs, feet and eyes should follow. What is the general shape of the bird? How big is it? Try to compare the size with a more familiar species such as a sparrow, starling, blackbird, jackdaw or herring gull. How does it walk and fly? When it is flying does it reveal any characteristic marks or shapes on the wing or tail? Try to make notes on the song and call.

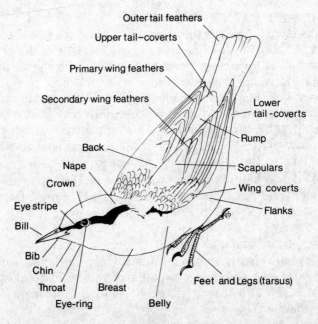

So far you have been describing the bird and how it behaves. An equally important point is to make field notes on where the bird is found — at the edge of the wood; in the centre of the wood; on the ground; on a trunk or in the canopy. When did you see it — what time of year and day?

In most bird species only the male sings. One reason for singing is to tell other birds of the same species that he 'owns' a territory. He will defend this against other birds and will use it for nesting and for finding food for his mate and offspring. You will find it difficult to identify some bird songs as many birds have a wide range of different calls — it will take years of patient listening to be able to sort them all out! The great tit, for example, has at least nineteen variations of song and many more calls.

There are several good records of bird song. Try to borrow some and listen to the differences in songs before you go into the wood. Concentrate on sorting out one or two songs first, then, when you have learned them and can identify them in the wood, add another couple of songs to your list.

THE LIFE CYCLE OF A BIRD

Birds have life cycles that vary from under one year to many years. An example of a short life cycle is that of the great tit, which lives for about 1½ years. Eggs hatch in the spring, the young develop, they learn how to fly and how to find their own food. Feathers become bedraggled and the bird will moult and grow new ones before the next breeding season begins. The bird then finds himself a new territory and another mate. They then build a nest together and the eggs are laid — thus the cycle starts again.

This will happen several times during the life of the bird. Some larger birds, such as the larger birds of prey, take more than a year to reach breeding condition.

BIRDS IN WOODS

The main factors that determine which birds are found in each type of wood are: woodland structure; food supply; nest sites and cover from predators and from severe weather.

This means that you can study woodland birds from the point of view of woodland structure or from that of the dominant tree species. It is very probable that the structure of the wood is as important, if not more important, to birds than the type of trees growing there.

If we consider woodland structure first, we find that some birds prefer open canopy woodlands, while others prefer a closed canopy, a well-developed shrub layer or a poor shrub layer and a poor, scattered herb layer. Herons and rooks, for example, favour closed canopy woodlands for breeding.

Birds that catch insects on the wing — spotted flycatcher, pied flycatcher and redstart — like open woodlands. The green woodpecker likes open woodlands with plenty of short herbs or grasses because it spends much of its time feeding on grassland insects.

Some birds like a well-developed under-storey or a good tall shrub layer. Birds that nest in such conditions are the song thrush, blackbird, greenfinch, redpoll, wood pigeon, turtle-dove, collared dove, jay and, in many situations, the magpie.

A Jay at the nest

A Woodland Owl — The Tawny Owl

A good shrub and herb layer is used for both feeding and nesting by such birds as blackcap, garden warbler, whitethroat, wren, chiffchaff, willow warbler, robin and long tailed tit.

Two kinds of birds nest in the holes of trees: those that make their own holes, like the green woodpecker, the great spotted woodpecker and the lesser spotted woodpecker; and those that use natural holes in trees. There are many of these, among which are the goosander, the tawny owl and barn owl, stock dove, jackdaw, great tit, blue tit, coal tit, marsh tit, redstart, pied flycatcher and starling. The willow tit makes its own nest hole, but only in soft rotten wood. The nuthatch is halfway between the two groups, as it will often alter the shape of an existing hole. Occasionally some birds will take over the nest hole of another species — for example, nuthatches have been seen evicting great tits from their holes, and starlings have evicted great spotted woodpeckers.

The lack of suitable nest sites is often a limiting factor. In many woods the number of pied flycatchers has been dramatically increased by the provision of additional nest sites in the form of nest boxes.

Some species of birds show a preference for woods containing dominant species of trees. For example, wood warblers show a preference for beech in south-eastern England and for oak in Wales. The capercaillie and crested tit like the pine forests of the central Highlands. Crossbills and siskins are largely birds of the conifer forest, while the lesser spotted woodpecker is perhaps most common where there is plenty of ash.

SOME IDEAS FOR STUDYING BIRDS IN WOODS
Choose two or three distinctive species, such as the robin, coal tit, blackbird or green woodpecker. Do these birds occur throughout the wood, only at the edges or only where certain types of tree grow? Do they occur where the wood is thickest or where it is most open? You will soon discover quite a lot about the habits of your woodland birds by systematic recordings of this sort. Where do you normally see redwings, or thrushes or blackbirds? Do the tits and goldcrests use a different part of the wood? Have you got redpolls in your wood and, if so, where do you usually find them?

Try to note if birds are in the tree tops, on areas of open ground within the wood, or under extensive cover afforded by bramble, hawthorn or shrub and under-storey layers. Note whether birds are most common in the centre of the wood or in border hedges. You may be lucky enough to distinguish some patterns of movement in changing weather conditions.

The time of year affects how you should go about watching birds. For example in spring most birds are scattered throughout the wood and wherever you start you are likely to come across some bird species. After the breeding season is over, many birds tend to flock together and will move through the wood in a noisy party. At this time the best thing to do is to walk slowly and quietly through the wood listening for feeding parties of tits or finches.

You could, for example, study the woodland from the point of view of one bird such as the great spotted woodpecker. First find the woodpecker, then watch it closely and note down what you see. Does it feed on all trees or does it just select a few to feed on? Does it fly from one tree to the next or does it miss out several trees? Are all the trees on which it feeds of the same species? Does it start feeding at the bottom of a tree and work upwards or does it start halfway up? Do you ever see the bird working downwards along the trunk or branch? Does it live mainly in the centre of a wood or does it use trees along the edges just as frequently? You can ask yourself dozens of questions like these and try to find some answers. Or you may prefer to start by making notes. Whichever way you go about it you will find that you are not only studying the woodpecker but also finding out quite a lot of information about the wood itself.

Birds cough up pellets or castings that contain the remains of indigestible parts of their food, such as the skulls and bones of birds and animals, the wing cases of beetles, the fur of mammals, or husks of seed. If you find the pellets of a bird such as the tawny owl, you can tease out the pellet with two needles and discover what animals the bird has been feeding upon. You can search the ground beneath a rookery for rook castings. Some people think that the rook plays quite an important part in bringing nutrients into the woods where it has nest colonies.

When studying birds you must be careful not to disturb them. Herons, for example, are suspicious of human beings and can easily be disturbed; so it is unwise to pay more than one or two short visits to a wood where they are nesting. If you do upset them, they may leave their nests and never return.

HOW TO DISCOVER BIRD TERRITORIES

The common-bird census mapping technique was designed by the population section of the British Trust for Ornithology and based on a technique used by Anders Enemar. By using symbols to plot different types of bird activity on a map you can find out the extent of each bird territory.

In the first instance you should select only a small area of woodland. About 2 hectares, or an area 100 metres by 100 metres, will be big enough for your first territory maps. Once you have become familiar with the methods you may wish to try something a little larger — say 5 hectares or more.

This technique is used for a breeding-bird census and counts should be made between mid-March (or a little later if the spring is cold) and the end of June. Visits should be made in fine weather when birds are singing — early morning is a very good time. You should try to make two or three visits a week until you have been nine to twelve times.

A large-scale map or sketch map is required (a 25 inch to the mile Ordnance Survey map is ideal). You will need one map for each visit plus other maps for showing the final distribution of each bird species (or one map could be used for two visits if a pen of a different colour is used for each visit).

Each visit should have a code letter (Visit A, Visit B, Visit C etc). Write this on the top of the map together with the date and time of the survey, as well as other useful information such as the weather conditions and the length of the visit.

Each bird should be recorded at the exact spot on the map by using the accepted code letters for each species and a symbol that shows its behaviour.

Symbols used (the examples given are for the blackbird).

Ⓑ	singing male
<u>B</u>	alarm call
B material	seen with nest material in beak
B food	seen with food in beak
BB	two males fighting (movement of either on breaking up can be shown by an arrow)
B*	nest
B	sight of bird

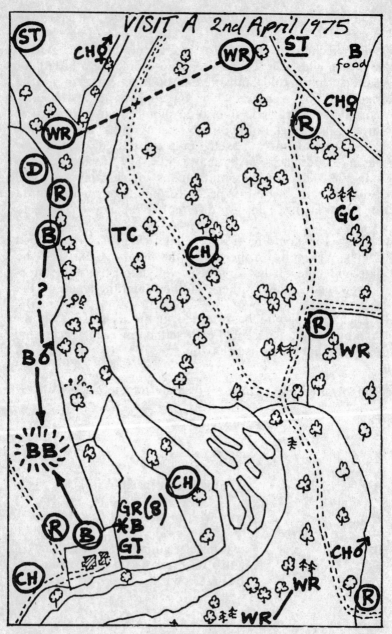

MAP SHOWING DISTRIBUTION OF BIRDS.   VISIT A

102

B ♂   sight of male

B ♀   sight of female

B Juv   sight of juvenile

Ⓑ ———————— Ⓑ   different males singing at same time

B♂ ———————— B♂   different birds in view at the same time

Ⓑ ——————— Ⓑ   singing bird seen to fly to a new position

CODE FOR BIRD SPECIES

B	Blackbird	MA	Mallard
BC	Blackcap	MG	Magpie
BF	Bullfinch	MT	Marsh tit
BT	Blue tit	N	Nightingale
BZ	Buzzard	NH	Nuthatch
C	Carrion crow	PF	Pied flycatcher
CC	Chiffchaff	PH	Pheasant
CD	Collared dove	R	Robin
CH	Chaffinch	RT	Redstart
CT	Coal tit	SD	Stock dove
D	Dunnock	SG	Starling
G	Green woodpecker	SH	Sparrowhawk
GC	Goldcrest	ST	Song thrush
GR	Greenfinch	TC	Treecreeper
GS	Great spotted woodpecker	TD	Turtle-dove
GT	Great tit	TO	Tawny owl
GW	Garden warbler	TP	Tree pipit
HF	Hawfinch	TS	Tree sparrow
J	Jay	WH	Whitethroat
K	Kestrel	WK	Woodcock
LO	Little owl	WO	Wood warbler
LS	Lesser spotted woodpecker	WR	Wren
LT	Long-tailed tit	WT	Willow tit
M	Mistle-thrush	WW	Willow warbler

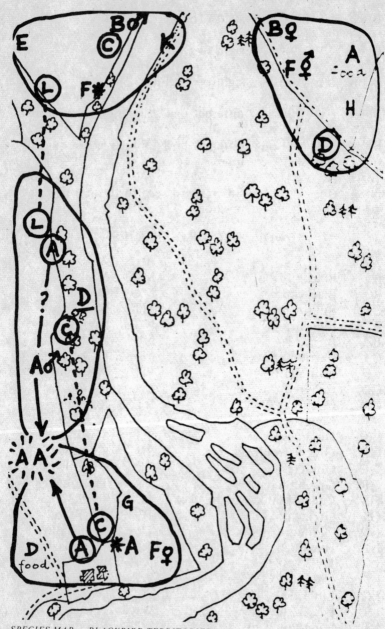

SPECIES MAP — BLACKBIRD TERRITORIES
(Each letter represents 4 Blackbird sightings for each visit)

For birds that nest in 'colonies', such as rooks, herons, greenfinches and tree sparrows, use the accepted symbol and the number of birds seen at each visit. For example GR(8) would mean eight greenfinches, which would probably represent four nesting pairs.

Starlings are best counted when the nestlings are noisy.

When you have completed all your visits arrange the maps in order, (A, B, C, D etc). To prepare species maps that will show the individual territories of one species — for example the blackbird — work through your visit maps in order and transfer all the information on the blackbird from the Visit A map to the species map. Put a pencil line through those observations that you have transferred to the species map. Do the same for Visit B, then Visit C, and so on until you have covered all your visits.

The visit records will probably stand out in groups of symbols and each group will probably represent the extent of a territory.

You can see whether the territories are evenly distributed through the wood, or round its edge, or whether they are associated with particular kinds of trees.

STUDYING MIGRATION

If you can visit a woodland regularly it may be worth recording the kinds and numbers of birds you see during the first ten minutes of each visit. If you make histograms with your results you may be able to detect movements of birds in and out of your chosen wood. These movements are particularly marked in autumn and spring.

Ornithologists learn about migration of birds by trapping them, placing a light aluminium ring on their legs and then releasing them again. Each ring contains a number and an address. If somebody finds a dead bird with a ring on or re-catches one in a net or trap, he is requested to send the ring number to the address on the ring. In this way ornithologists learn about birds' movement, migration and the length of birds' lives.

12
INVERTEBRATES IN WOODS

Some groups of insects are difficult to identify, but it is not necessary to describe all the species you find. The more experience you have the more familiar you will become with certain groups and you may then be able to identify some of them down to species level. In the first instance make lists of animals — such as woodlice, centipedes, dragonflies, butterflies, moths and beetles. A list showing the presence or absence of the major groups of invertebrate animals makes a good start.

Moths such as the puss moth and poplar hawk are easy to identify. Butterflies such as the marbled white, the orange tip and the brimstone are also easy to recognize. You should also be able to identify ladybirds, weevils, timber men, ground beetles, dor beetles, earwigs, shield bugs and capsid bugs.

If your interest is in insects remember that different insects are on the wing in different months and that each species of insect will be at a different stage of its development depending on the time of year. In many ways the insect situation is not unlike that of flowers, with a changing pattern throughout the year.

MOTHS AND BUTTERFLIES
If you are interested in moths and butterflies, woods are excellent places to begin your study as about half of all the British species are found in woodlands. The larvae (caterpillars) of over one hundred kinds of butterfly and moth feed on oak leaves, and hawthorn and sallow also make very popular food.

Several species of butterfly and moth occur over a large part of Britain. Examples are the large poplar hawk moth, and the green-veined white and purple hairstreak butterflies. At the other extreme, the Kentish glory is now found only in the Wye Forest in England and near Aviemore in Scotland. This large, beautiful white-and-chestnut moth can be found flying on the first warm days in April. Several other forests have their own species: the scarce hook tip is found only in the Forest of Dean, and the black hairstreak is confined to a few blackthorn thickets in central England.

Before setting out to learn about butterflies and moths you will have to give careful thought to the methods of tackling the problem. There are two problems: first butterflies and moths are found on the wing for only very limited periods of time, and second they may be distributed over a limited area. You should also understand the life histories of the group, details of which follow.

THE LIFE CYCLE OF THE BUTTERFLY AND MOTH

Butterfly and moth eggs hatch into caterpillars and these shed their skins several times as they grow. The caterpillar eventually changes into a pupa, a sedentary stage in which the adult insect develops. The adult insect eventually hatches from the pupa, and finds a mate, and then the cycle starts again. The cycle occurs at different times of the year with different moths and butterflies: some pass the winter as an egg while other pass the winter in the caterpillar, pupa or adult stage.

STUDYING BUTTERFLIES AND MOTHS

Moths and butterflies all have their own preferences for different types of tree, different parts of a wood or a different part of the country. It is interesting to compare the types of butterflies and moths found in broad-leaved woodlands with those found in conifer woods.

If you go into a wood without preparation you may be disappointed. You need an insect book (see the list on page 122), for plotting on a bar chart those months when various insects can be found on the wing. Write a list of species down the left-hand margin of the page and the months of the year along the bottom. Then draw a line level with the species to cover the months in which it is found flying. You can then either look for very definite species when you go into the wood or select a month in which a lot of species are likely to be on the wing. Some distinctive or common woodland butterflies you could start with are: green-veined white, wood white, speckled wood, ringlet, brimstone, comma, silver-washed fritillary, high-brown fritillary, pearl-bordered fritillary, small pearl-bordered fritillary and chequered skipper.

The next point to notice is that these butterflies, and the same applies to moths, will usually be found in woods that contain a fair amount of the special plant food for their caterpillars. So in addition to looking at a likely month it is advisable to note the plant food that attracts these insects. Again a good insect or butterfly book will be essential.

You will also need a distribution map of the species you are looking for. For example it is no good looking for brimstones in Scotland or some of the fritillaries in eastern England. The Biological Records Centre (address on page 124) is now producing distribution maps of many species and there are also maps in the appropriate volumes in the *New Naturalist* series published by Collins.

Your problems are not over yet, because butterflies and moths have very definite preferences for different parts of the wood. Usually, but not always, most butterflies enjoy open canopy woodland or rides.

Even if you have prepared your plan of attack carefully, you will still not come across many moths, because moths usually fly at night. But you need not necessarily stumble

Lime Hawk Moth

Brimstone butterfly

about the wood at night in order to find your moths. Moths rest by day and can occasionally be found on the trunks of trees, particularly those that have an irregular bark, such as the oak. Moths and butterflies are easily disturbed by wind, so they often rest on the sheltered side of a branch or tree trunk or will be found under banks, walls or rocks. They are likely to be well hidden or camouflaged, as birds will be looking for moths to eat. Apart from colouring, moths use several ingenious methods of hiding themselves from predators. The buff tip moth, for example, rolls its wings to look like a twig.

You should not confine your search for butterflies and moths to the adult insects. Many caterpillars are spectacular and worth looking for. Caterpillars tend to like the young fresh leaves at the tips of shoots and can often be found there. The caterpillars of the larger moths such as the poplar hawk or the puss moth are relatively easy to keep in captivity. It is fascinating to watch them change from one stage to another and then emerge from their pupa. However, they need a lot of care and attention: fresh leaves daily, the right humidity and temperature and somewhere to pupate.

If a female hatches you can then attract a male to it and start the cycle all over again. You will probably have very many more caterpillars than you require through breeding in this way and these can be put on to suitable food plants locally, thereby helping to conserve the population of the insect.

You will probably come across some pupae when you carry out a close search of your woodland. Some butterfly pupae will be found attached to the plant food while others will be found in many hiding places, such as crevices or cracks in bark, or in the soil at the base of a tree or shrub.

OTHER INSECTS

Many hundreds of other insects spend some or all of their time on trees and on their leaves and you could begin a long, detailed and interesting study of the animals associated with one tree alone.

A careful search of the soil is always an interesting exercise as you will find not only the odd pupae but many other types of animal. Beetles, beetle larvae, centipedes, millipedes and worms are a few examples.

One of the largest orders of insects is the beetle. There are so many types of beetles that on almost any excursion into a woodland you should find some, or at any rate their larvae.

Beetles of one kind or another can be found almost anywhere at any time of year. Many species feed on decaying animal or plant matter and so corpses and animal dung are two good places to search for beetles. They will also be found on dead or dying leaves, on fungi, in moss and vegetation, and on the branches and leaves of trees.

Many other orders of insects, such as grasshoppers, earwigs, froghoppers and greenfly, flies and a wide range of bees, wasps, ants and ichneumon can also be found in woods. Wood ants and wood wasps are particularly spectacular examples.

On the twigs or leaves of many trees you may see some unusual growths called galls. There are many types of galls and they form all kinds and shapes of growth. The best known are probably the oak apple and oak marble gall. The oak apple is not an apple or a fruit of any kind, but the home of a tiny grub that will eventually hatch out into a gall wasp. Gall wasps on oak often hatch out in September or October. You can tell if there is a gall wasp inside an oak marble because when it leaves it makes a tiny hole on the outside of the gall. If there is no hole the gall wasp grub should still be inside.

Dragonflies are not normally considered to be woodland insects as they breed in water. But many species of dragonfly will use the more open parts of a woodland near water for feeding or resting. Species such as the hairy dragonfly *Brachytron pratense* and some *Aeshna* species are often found in woods on warm sunny days. Several species of dragonfly breed in peat bogs and these may be seen in the more open type of birch woodlands of the Highlands.

OTHER INVERTEBRATES
Woods make fine habitats for spiders and on a nice bright sunny morning you may see a mass of glistening webs. If the woodland habitat contains a very large number of insects, it is not surprising that the predatory spider will be common in the same habitat. If you look at a spider's web you will frequently see a number of different kinds of insects trapped there.

A CODE FOR INSECT COLLECTING
A code with a large number of points of interest and importance has been prepared by the Joint Committee for the Conservation of British Insects. There are thirty-five points arranged in six general headings:

    collecting — general
    collecting — rare and endangered species
    collecting — lights and light traps
    collecting — permission and conditions
    collecting — damage to environment
    breeding

Copies of the code can be obtained from:

    Joint Committee for the Conservation of British Insects,
      Royal Entomoligical Society,
        41 Queen's Gate,
          London SW7.

13
MAN AND WOODS

From evidence provided by fossils we know that many millions of years ago most trees and forests in Britain were very different from those we know today. Not only were trees different to look at but the animals that roamed through the forests were also different. These were the ages of dinosaurs and pterodactyls. Such forests have long disappeared under new rocks and have been compressed and hardened, so that many of them now form those rather special rocks that we know as coal. By looking at an atlas to see where coalfields are found today, you can get a good idea where the forests were in prehistoric times. Many museums display fossil plants from these early times and you will be able to consult books for photographs of fossils and reconstructed drawings of how scientists think the forests looked.

Between twenty and ten thousand years ago much of Britain was covered by ice. Then slowly the climate became warmer and the ice melted, leaving the ground strewn with boulders, rock, pebbles and clay. In many parts of Britain today you can see the results of the Ice Age and the retreat of the glaciers. Large boulders of one kind of rock were moved by ice over the ground and left standing on top of a completely different type of rock. Sharp boulders and rocks scratched and cut lines in the underlying rock as the ice moved them over rock surfaces. Many of these lines can still be seen today. In many places great banks or cliffs of boulder clay contain many kinds of rocks carried from far-off places by moving ice sheets. So ten thousand years ago much of Britain was left in a desolate and barren state, devoid of trees and vegetation.

You can also look for a different type of evidence that will reveal secrets about old woodlands after the Ice Age. If you are walking over northern or western hills you may be lucky enough to come across the remains of trees in eroded peat. In many places where the river authorities cut through deep beds of peat or other soils to make drainage ditches they come across the remains of old forest trees embedded and preserved in peat. If you get an opportunity to look at some of these drainage channels you may find chunks or branches of birch trees that have been preserved for many hundreds of thousands of years in peat. When marshes are drained for agricultural purposes, you often find large trunks of 'bog oak' from former times. You can discover only odd fragments of information about our prehistoric woodlands from information gained from such scattered remains. But other remains give more information.

Wind-pollinated trees and shrubs such as oak, birch, alder, pine and hazel produce a very large quantity of pollen grains. Most of the pollen grains are wasted and eventually fall on to the ground but if the ground is an acid peat bog, they are preserved, as very little decay takes place in peat bogs. Now it so happens that each type of tree has a pollen grain that is quite different from that of any other type of tree. In 1934 Professor Godwin of Cambridge University described how you could look at layer upon layer of peat deposits and discover, from the pollen grains in each layer, which trees were growing during the period in which each deposit was formed. From such 'pollen analysis' we can build up a very accurate picture of which trees were growing in a district at any particular time and what changes took place.

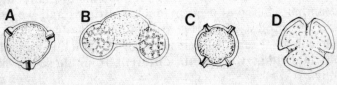

Pollen grains magnified about 500 times
A Birch   B Pine   C Alder   D Oak

The story that pollen analysis tells is that the climate was, in the period after the Ice Age, much cooler than today. Trees that are today found in cool northern latitudes then covered much of Britain. Birch, juniper and willow were some of the first trees to appear after the ice retreated. Warmer climates followed and the ice cover continued to

113

melt and retreat towards the north, leaving bare ground and patches of soil. Trees then spread northwards over Britain. After the birch woods had become established, pine trees took over, thanks to the warmer climate. In some places oak, ash, elm and hazel appeared where conditions were suitable. Elsewhere beech, lime and hornbeams dominated the woodlands and in wet areas alder flourished. Thus over a period of several thousand years the landscape in Britain was continually changing.

About seven thousand years ago the climate became much wetter and the evidence from peat-pollen analysis suggests that in much of the western and northern parts of Britain the number of forest trees was reduced as much of the ground became waterlogged, and bogs and mires formed.

During the next five thousand years a warm wet period, in which alder, oak, elm and lime dominated the landscape, was followed by a warm dry period with a very mixed forest cover. A cooler wetter period came next with beech, hornbeam, alder, oak, elm and birch prominent. Limes declined in this period.

We also know that shortly before the birth of Christ much of Britain was covered by a mixture of broad-leaved deciduous forests.

CHANGING WOODLAND ANIMALS

Animal species that lived in the forest also changed. Archaeologists have discovered the remains of many different animals in caves used by ancient Britons and we know from examples of early art and from decoration of archaeological remains that many of the animals hunted by man in Britain were quite different from those we have today.

We can date archaeological remains by means of a process discovered by William F. Libby in the United States in 1949. Libby used radioactive carbon 14, which is formed by cosmic rays in the atmosphere. Carbon 14 is accumulated in plants that are eventually eaten by animals and man. When the plant or animal dies the radioactive carbon in wood or in bones slowly breaks down. Libby discovered that after 5,500 years only half the radioactive carbon that had been there when the plant or animal died was left. After another 5,500 years there was only half as much again. This means that measuring the amount of radioactive carbon we can get a rough idea of the age of the wood or bone. Scientists have also been able to compare the dates given from radio-carbon dating with the sequence of events found by other methods such as pollen analysis or by the examination of remains found in various layers in the floors of prehistoric buildings or caves.

By using radio-carbon dating, scientists have learned that in the earliest part of the Old Stone Age in Britain, which goes back to between 500,000 and 40,000 BC (Lower and Middle Palaeolithic periods), woolly rhinoceroses, mammoths and reindeer were wandering over Britain, while in warmer spells between the Ice Ages elephants and rhinoceroses were found. Elephants presumably fed on the leaves of trees in much the same way as they do in Africa and India today. In caves in Denbighshire (now Clwyd) and the Gower Peninsula in Wales the remains of bones of mammoth, woolly rhinoceros, elk, hyaena and cave bear, dating from the later part of the Old Stone Age, have been found. These animals were probably hunted by the men living in those areas at that time. Some caves in Derbyshire have drawings that include the heads of horses, and reindeer, which suggests that these animals probably roamed the country between 40,000 and 10,000 BC. Then forests spread over Britain and animals such as wild pig, elk, red deer, wolf, brown bear, and wild cat were found.

So far we have discussed three main groups of animals: those that died out as a result of major changes in the climate; those that were killed off or made extinct in Britain by man, such as the wild pig, elk, wolf, and brown bear, and those, such as the red deer and wild cat, that still exist.

THE USE OF FORESTS BY MAN

Much of Britain was covered by trees when man came from Europe to settle here. From the days when we can first trace evidence of man in Britain he has been dependent upon wood and woods for many of his daily needs.

During the first few thousand years of man's existence he

was a hunter and much of his food was found in the forest. He hunted wild boar and deer living there and also gathered the fruits that he found.

Over a long period of time he changed from being a hunter to being a farmer. For this new way of life he needed to clear the forest so that he could make fields for grazing domesticated animals or for growing crops. Fields would usually be small and often surrounded by trees.

These early farmers were probably careless with the land. If the soil became poor or overworked or was washed away in a flood, the farmer simply cleared away some more forest. Clearing was done in a number of ways, depending on the place, the time of year and the type of forest. Burning would quickly destroy some of the pine forests or much of the scrub woodland. If there were a lot of scattered birch trees a polished stone axe-head would probably be capable of clearing suitable areas of forest in a fairly short time. In a recent experiment in Denmark over a hundred birch trees were felled with an axe-head that had not been sharpened for about four thousand years! Once the trees had been cleared man's grazing animals, particularly goats, would help to keep the area free from trees by eating the young seedlings. Wild boars and domesticated pigs would search for acorns and this would prevent many seeds from growing into young trees, to replace those that had been felled or had died of old age.

On heavier and damper soils of the lowlands large oak woodlands, being of harder wood, were more difficult to clear with primitive implements. But here again man's grazing animals, such as sheep, goats and cattle, could nibble off the young tender seedlings and thus prevent many of the trees from reaching maturity.

Once the destruction of the forests had started it continued at an increasing rate. Man increasingly needed land for cultivation and for grazing his domestic animals. He also required wood for fires and later turned some of this into charcoal for smelting. By the Middle Ages timber was being used widely, for most houses were made of wood, only the larger houses and castles being made of stone. The Great Fire of London in 1666 spread quickly because so many buildings were timber. Many black-and-white wooden Tudor buildings can still be seen today.

Woodlands kept on disappearing at a steady pace as wood continued to be the major raw material used in Britain. For many centuries timber continued to be one of the main materials used for house building. It was also used for shipbuilding, for household goods and tools, and for heating homes. The bark of the oak tree was essential for tanning leather and several types of wood were used for making charcoal for the early smelting industry. So more and more trees were cut down — but very few trees were planted to replace them.

In the early days of the Industrial Revolution fuel was urgently required by factories. The rapid growth of the iron industry in South Wales was largely due to the availability of ironstone, wood and limestone, all of which were essential for making iron. Woodlands soon became extremely important to industry. Most of the valleys in South Wales had well-wooded hillsides, which helped the growth of the iron industry. Soon several other forest areas began to produce iron: the Forest of Dean, many woodland areas round Birmingham, and the Forest of Arden, for example.

By the middle of the eighteenth century, when iron furnaces began to use coke instead of charcoal, much of the valley woodlands had already disappeared. In many other valleys smoke, with high concentrations of sulphur dioxide and other gases, severely affected the growth of new trees. Yet man's need for woodlands continued. By the nineteenth century pit props were required in large numbers for mines, and timber was required for railway building. Timber was still being used without much thought of replanting or controlling forests. As a result by the middle of the nineteenth century vast areas of Britain that had once been covered by woodland were now farmland, wasteland or industrial land.

In the twentieth century two world wars caused further reduction in our woodlands. Home-grown timber was urgently required for a wide range of uses. It was too risky to bring wood into the country by cargo boat because of enemy torpedoes, so as much wood as possible was felled in Britain. As we have seen, in 1919, after the First World War, the government decided to plant more trees to meet our timber requirements. It was then that the Forestry Commission was formed.

Although many private landowners were by now beginning to plant their own woodlands, it was not until the foundation of the Forestry Commission that planting was carried out on a large scale in many parts of the country. There was one big change in Britain's new woodlands: the government wanted trees to grow quickly so large numbers of quick-growing conifers were planted. Thus a country that had once been covered with deciduous broad-leafed trees was now being planted with exotic softwood trees. Landowners with areas of land that are too poor for good agricultural use also frequently plant quick-growing, softwood forests. Most of the forests grown by large, private organizations, such as the Economic Forestry Group, are conifer forests.

Careful management of the forest is required if it is to produce a good crop of timber. In some of the broad-leaved hardwood forests different forms of management, such as pollarding and coppicing, are carried out. In pollarding, trees are cut about 2–3 metres above the ground and the trunk then produces a large number of branches. These branches are very suitable for fencing and basketry. In East Anglia, in particular, you will frequently see lines of pollarded willows along roadsides and drainage ditches. Famous examples of pollards include the hornbeams in Epping Forest and Burnham Beeches in Buckinghamshire. Coppicing is the result of a similar process, but here trees are felled at the base and fast-growing shoots spring up from the cut. Hazel, oak, ash and alder all produce shoots after felling. Coppicing is particularly common in Kent and on the Weald. After a few years the young shoots provide ideal hop poles and fencing materials. Coppiced woodland is particularly favoured by the best known of our song birds — the nightingale. As the art of coppicing is gradually dying out we may experience a drop in the number of nightingales in southern Britain.

Standard oaks with coppiced hazel

FOR FURTHER READING

The following books are general works on woodlands or woodland plants and animals. They deal in greater detail with many of the features or topics discussed in this book. Most of these books should be available through your library.

Books for the beginner

Hadfield, M. (1964) Your book of trees. Faber.
Hadfield, M. (1970) Discovering England's trees. Shire Publications.
Jackman, L. (1970) Exploring the woodland. Evans Brothers.
Vesey Fitzgerald, B. (1963) Trees. Ladybird book. Wills and Hepworth.

CHAPTER 1 THE WORLD OF THE WOOD
Clapham, A. R., Tutin, T. G. and Warburg, E. F. (1952) Flora of the British Isles. Cambridge University Press. (Advanced).
Miles, P. M. and Miles, H. B. (1968) Woodland ecology. Hulton's Biological Field Studies. Hulton.
Neal, E. (1953) Woodland ecology. Heinemann.
Steele, R. E. and Welch, R. C. (1973) Monks Wood. A Nature Reserve Record. The Nature Conservancy. (Advanced).
Tansley, A. G. (1962) Introduction to plant ecology. Allen and Unwin.
Willis, A. J. (1973) Introduction to plant ecology. Allen and Unwin.

CHAPTER 2 THE WOODLAND YEAR
Batten, L. et al (1973) Birdwatchers' year. Poyser.

CHAPTER 3 HOW TO BEGIN TO STUDY A WOODLAND
Berks, Bucks and Oxon Naturalists' Trust. Projects for environmental studies.
Brown, V. (1960) The amateur naturalist's handbook. Faber.
Clarke, E. (1973) Fieldwork in biology. Macmillan.
Clarke, G. R. The study of soil in the field. Oxford University Press.
Evan, I. O. (1949) The observer's book of British geology. Warne.
Ford, V. E. (1959) How to begin your field work: woodland. Murray.
Goodfellow, P. Projects with birds. David and Charles.
Harris, R. (1969) Natural history collecting. Hamlyn.
Heath, J. and Scott, D. (1972) Instructions for recorders. Biological Records Centre.
Knight, M. (1966) Field work for young naturalists. Bell.
Newing, F. E. and Bowood, R. (1962) The weather. Ladybird. Wills and Hepworth.
Reade, W. and Stuttard, R. M. Eds. (1968) A handbook for naturalists. Evans Brothers.
Scott, N. (1967) Understanding maps. Ladybird. Wills and Hepworth.
Watson, G. G. (1967) Junior naturalists handbook. Piccolo.

CHAPTER 4 CLOTHING AND EQUIPMENT
Flegg, J. J. M. (1972) Binoculars, telescopes and cameras for the birdwatcher. British Trust for Ornithologists. Field Guide No. 14.

CHAPTER 5 WHAT IS A TREE?
Edlin, H. L. (1973) Trees and timbers. Routledge and Kegan Paul.
Edlin, H. L. and Nimmo, M. (1956) Treasury of trees. Countrygoer Press.
Kosch, A. (1964) The young specialist looks at trees. Burke.
Mackean. D. G. (1962) Introduction to biology. Murray.
Morris, M. G. and Perring. F. H. (1974) The British oak. Classey. (Advanced)

CHAPTER 6   IDENTIFYING TREES

Edlin, H. L. (1964) Wayside and woodland trees. Warne.

Edlin, H. L. (1968) Know your broadleaves. Forestry Commission booklet, No. 20, HMSO.

Edlin, H. L. (1970) Know your conifers. Forestry Commission booklet No. 15, HMSO.

Martin, W. K. (1965) The concise British flora in colour. Ebury Press. Michael Joseph.

Mitchell, A. F. (1972) Conifers in the British Isles. Forestry Commission booklet No. 33, HMSO.

Mitchell, A. F. (1974) A field guide to the trees of Britain and Northern Europe. Collins.

Mitchell, A. F. and Williams J. (1973) Common trees. Forestry Commission booklet, No. 38, HMSO.

Nicholson, B. E., Ary, S. and Gregory, M. (1960) The Oxford book of wild flowers. Oxford University Press.

Stokoe, W. J. (1960) The observer's book of trees. Warne.

CHAPTER 7   WHAT IS A WOODLAND?

Bellamy, D. (1972) Bellamy on botany. BBC Publications.

Condry. W. (1974) Woodlands. Collins Countryside Series.

Hickin, N. E. (1971) The natural history of an English forest. Arrow Books.

Tansley, A. G. (1949) The British Isles and their vegetation. Cambridge. (Advanced)

Tubbs, C. R. (1968) The New Forest. David and Charles. (Advanced)

CHAPTER 8   LIVES OF WOODLAND PLANTS

Blamey, M., Fitter, R. and Fitter, A. (1974) The wild flowers of Britain and North-Western Europe. Collins Guides.

Fitter, R. S. R. (1971) Finding wild flowers. Collins Guides.

Gilmore, J. and Walters, M. (1954) Wildflowers. New Naturalist Series. Collins.

Prime, C. T. (1960) Lords and ladies. New Naturalist Monograph, Collins.

Proctor, M. and Yeo, P. (1973) The pollination of flowers. New Naturalist Series, Collins.

Turrill, W. B. (1948) British plant life. New Naturalist Series, Collins.

CHAPTER 9   FLOWERLESS PLANTS IN WOODS

Alvin, K. L. and Kershaw, K. A. (1963) The observer's book of lichens. Warne.

Brightman, F. H. and Nicholson, B. E. (1966) The Oxford book of flowerless plants. Oxford University Press.

Hyde, H. A., Wade, A. E. and Harrison, S. G. (1940) Welsh ferns, clubmosses, quillworts and horsetails. National Museum of Wales.

Jewell, A. L. (1955) The observer's book of mosses and liverworts. Warne.

Lange, M. and Hora, F. B. (1963) Collins Guide to mushrooms and toadstools. Collins.

Stokoe, W. J. (1965) The observer's book of ferns. Warne.

Wakefield, E. M. (1958) The observer's book of common fungi. Warne.

Watson, E. V. (1955) British mosses and liverworts. Cambridge University Press.

CHAPTER 10   LARGER ANIMALS IN WOODS

Cadman, W. A. (1966) The fallow deer. Forestry Commission leaflet No. 52, HMSO.

Council for Nature. (1973) Predatory mammals in Britain. (From Society for the Promotion of Nature Reserves.)

Hurrell, H. G. (1968) Pine Martens, Forestry Commission: Forest Record No. 64, HMSO.

Lawrence M. J. and Brown, R. W. (1967) Mammals of Britain — their tracks, trails and signs. Blandford.

Mathews, L. H. (1952) British mammals. New Naturalist Series, Collins.

Morris, P. (1970) Hedgehogs. Forestry Commission: Forest Record No. 77, HMSO.

Neal, E. (1948) The badger. New Naturalist Monograph, Collins.

Nixon, M. and Whiteley, D. (1972) Oxford Book of Vertebrates. Oxford University Press.

Poole, T. B. (1970) Polecats. Forestry Commission: Forest Record No. 76, HMSO.

Shorten, M. (1954) Squirrels. New Naturalist Monograph, Collins.

Smith, M. (1951) The British amphibians and reptiles. New Naturalist Series, Collins.

Southern, H. N. (1964) A handbook of British mammals. Blackwell Scientific Publications.

Stephen, D. (1963) Guide to watching wildlife. Collins.

Van den Brink, F. H. (1967) A field guide to the mammals of Britain and Europe. Collins.

CHAPTER 11   BIRDS IN WOODS

Campbell, B. (1964) Birds and woodlands. Forestry Commission leaflet No. 47, HMSO.

Conder, P. (1969) Birds of woods and hedges (with records). Nelson.

Devon Trust for Nature Conservation (1969) School projects in natural history. Volume 2.

Heinzel, H., Fitter, R.S.R. and Parslow, J. (1974) The birds of Britain and Europe. Collins Guides.

Lack, D. (1943) The life of the robin. Fontana.

Leigh Pemberton, J. (1968) Heath and woodland birds. Ladybird Series. Wills and Hepworth.

Peterson, R., Mountford, G. and Hollom, P.A.D. (1954) A field guide to the birds of Britain and Europe. Collins.

Simms, E. (1971) Woodland birds. New Naturalist Series, Collins.

Yapp, W. B. (1962) Birds and Woods. Oxford University Press.

CHAPTER 12   INVERTEBRATES IN WOODS

Beedham, G. E. (1972) Identification of the British mollusca. Hulton.

Bristowe, W. S. (1958) The world of spiders. New Naturalist Series, Collins.

Burton, J., Bee, J., Whiteley, D. and Parks, P. (1968) The Oxford book of insects. Oxford University Press.

Chinery, M. (1973) A field guide to the insects of Britain and Northern Europe. Collins.

Higgins, L. and Riley, N. (1970) Butterflies of Britain and Europe. Collins Guides.

Howarth, T. G., ed. (1973) South's British Butterflies. Warne.

Imms, A. D. (1947) Insect natural history. New Naturalist Series, Collins.

Linssen, E. F. and Newman, L. H. (1953) The observer's book of common insects and spiders. Warne.

Linssen, E. F. (1949) Beetles of the British Isles. Wayside and Woodland Series, 2 vols. Warne.

Manning, S. A. (1965) Butterflies, moths and other insects. Ladybird. Wills and Hepworth.

McMillan, N. F. (1968) British shells. Wayside and Woodland series. Warne.

Nichols, D., Cooke, J. A. L. and Whiteley, D. (1971) The Oxford book of invertebrates. Oxford University Press.

Robinson, T. C. (1968) Butterflies in woodlands. Forestry Commission: Record No. 65, HMSO.
Showell, R. (1972) Learning about insects and small animals. Ladybird. Wills and Hepworth.
South, R. (1961) The moths of the British Isles. Warne.
Step, E. (1932) Bees, ants and allied insects of the British Isles. Warne.
Stokoe, W. J. (1937) The observer's book of butterflies. Warne.

CHAPTER 13   MAN AND WOODS
Baron, W. M. M. (1971) Nature conservation. Methuen.
Crowe, S. (1966) Forestry in landscape. Forestry Commission booklet No. 18, HMSO.
Edlin, H. L. (1970) Trees, woods and man. New Naturalist Series, Collins.
Edlin, H. L. (1973) Woodland crafts of Britain. David and Charles.
Fleure, H. J. (1959) A natural history of man in Britain. New Naturalist Series, Collins.
Mathews J. R. (1955) Origin and distribution of British flora. Hutchinson.
Stamp, D. (1969) Nature conservation in Britain. New Naturalist Series, Collins.
Steele, R. C. (1972) Wildlife conservation in woodlands. Forestry Commission booklet No. 29, HMSO.
Wood, R. F. and Andersen, I. A. (1968) Forestry in the British scene. Forestry Commission booklet No. 24, HMSO.

SOME USEFUL ADDRESSES

Natural History Societies

Amateur Entomologists'
Society
23 Manor Way
North Harrow
Middlesex

Association of School
Natural History Societies
Wormholt Lodge
76A Wormholt Road
London W.12

Botanical Society of the British Isles
c/o Department of Botany
British Museum (Natural History)
Cromwell Road
London SW7 5BD
Enquiries to: White Cottage, Slinfold,
Horsham, Sussex RH13 7RG

The British Butterfly
Conservation Society
Over Compton
Sherborne
Dorset

British Deer Society
Whale Moor Head
Lowther S. Park
Penrith
Cumbria

British Ecological Society
Harvest House
62 London Road
Reading RG1 5HS

British Entomological and Natural
History Society
c/o The Alpine Club
74 South Audley Street
London W1

British Mycological Society
c/o Imperial College Field Station
Silwood Park
Sunninghill
Berks SL5 7PY

British Naturalists' Association
Willowfield
Boyneswood Road
Four Marks
Alton
Hants GU34 5EA

British Trust for
Conservation Volunteers
c/o Zoological Gardens
Regents Park
London NW1 4RY

British Trust for Entomology
Hope Department of
Entomology
University Museum
Oxford

British Trust for Ornithology
Beech Grove
Tring
Herts

The Conchological Society of Great
Britain and Ireland
Clonard Cottage
Rowlands Avenue
Hatch End
Middlesex

Council for Nature
Zoological Gardens
Regents Park
London NW1 4RY

Mammal Society of the
British Isles
62 London Road
Reading
Berks

Men of the Trees
Crawley Down
Crawley
Sussex

Royal Entomological Society
41 Queen's Gate
London SW7

Royal Society for the
Protection of Birds
The Lodge
Sandy
Beds SG19 2DL

Scottish Ornithologists' Club
Scottish Centre for Ornithology and
Bird Protection
21 Regent Terrace
Edinburgh

Scottish Wildlife Trust
8 Dublin Street
Edinburgh

Society for the Promotion of Nature
Reserves
The Green
Nettleham
Lincoln

Wildlife Observation Society
c/o Royal Society for the Prevention of
Cruelty to Animals
105 Jermyn Street
London SW1

Wildlife Youth Service of the World
Wildlife Fund
Wallington
Surrey

Young Ornithologists' Club
The Lodge
Sandy
Beds SG19 2DL

Government Organizations

Biological Records Centre
Monks Wood Experimental Station
Abbots Ripton
Huntingdon PE17 2LS

Forestry Commission
25 Savile Row
London W1X 2AY

Nature Conservancy Council
19 Belgrave Square
London SW1X 8PY

National Organizations

Field Studies Council
9 Devereux Court
Strand
London WC2

National Trust
42 Queen Anne's Gate
London SW1

Youth Hostels Association (England and Wales)
Trevelyan House
8 St Stephen's Hill
St Albans
Herts

Natural History Books

E. W. Classey Ltd
Park Road
Faringdon
Berks SN7 7DR

Collins Ltd
144 Cathedral Street
Glasgow G4 ONB

Wildlife Slides

The Slide Centre Ltd
Portman House
17 Brodrick Road
London SW17 7DZ

Natural History Equipment

P. K. Dutt and Co. Ltd
113 Lavender Hill
Tonbridge
Kent

Watkins and Doncaster
110 Park View Road
Welling
Kent

Binoculars, Telescopes etc.

Heron Optical Co. Ltd
25 Kings Road
Brentwood
Essex

Metwood Accessories
Broadacre
Little Linford Road
Haversham
Nr. Wolverton
Bucks

Opticron (Dept. B)
400 Hatfield Road
St Albans
Herts

Recording Equipment

Sonic Instruments Ltd
10 Sunderton Lane
Clanfield
Hants
PO8 ONU

Clothing

J. Barbour and Sons Ltd
Simonside
South Shields
Co. Durham
NE34 9PD

Functional
20 Chepstow Street
Manchester M1 5JF

Husky of Tostock Ltd
Box D 23
115 Bury Street
Stowmarket
Suffolk

John Norris
21 Victoria Road
Penrith
Cumbria
CA11 8HP

CODES

Country Code

Guard against fire risks
Fasten all gates
Keep dogs under proper control
Keep to paths across farm land
Avoid damaging fences, hedges and walls
Leave no litter
Safeguard water supplies
Protect wildlife, wild plants and trees
Go carefully on country roads
Respect the life of the countryside.

Wildlife Code

Leave wild places as you find them
Leave wildlife in the wild
Disturbance may mean death
Take notes and photographs — not specimens
Leave wildflowers for others to enjoy
Observe bye-laws and codes of behaviour
Follow the country code.

Outdoor Studies Code

Plan and lead excursions well
Take safety seriously
Choose and use your area carefully
Respect ownership
Think of other users of the countryside
Leave the area as you found it
Avoid disturbing plants and animals
Do not collect unnecessarily
Safeguard rare species
Give no one cause to regret your visit.

Photographer's Code

The law as it affects nature photography must be observed
The welfare of the subject is more important than the photograph
Obtain permission first
Keep disturbance to a minimum.

LEAFLETS giving more details about codes can be obtained from the following:

COUNTRY CODE
Countryside Commission
John Dower House
Cheltenham
Glos

WILDLIFE CODE
Society for the Promotion of Nature Reserves
The Green
Nettleham
Lincoln

OUTDOOR STUDIES CODE
Field Studies Council
9 Devereux Court
Strand
London WC2

A CODE FOR INSECT COLLECTING
Joint Committee for the Conservation of British Insects
The Royal Entomological Society
41 Queen's Gate
London SW7

BOTANICAL SOCIETY OF THE BRITISH ISLES'
CODE OF CONDUCT
Botanical Society of the British Isles
c/o Department of Botany
British Museum (Natural History)
Cromwell Road
London SW7 5BD

NATURE PHOTOGRAPHERS' CODE OF PRACTICE and also WILD BIRDS
AND THE LAW
The Royal Society for the Protection of Birds
The Lodge
Sandy
Beds SG19 2DL

ACKNOWLEDGEMENTS

Line drawings by Peter Schofield except for page 89 — Susan Neale.

All photographs by Elizabeth and Anthony Bomford except for pages 9 and 97 — RJC Blewitt (ARDEA); page 62 — Peter Schofield; and page 65 based on a Nature Conservancy picture.